ANTHROPOLOGICAL PAPERS OF
THE UNIVERSITY OF ARIZONA

NUMBER 11

WILLIAM H. HODGE

THE ALBUQUERQUE NAVAJOS

THE UNIVERSITY OF ARIZONA PRESS

TUCSON 1969

THE UNIVERSITY OF ARIZONA PRESS

Copyright © 1969
The Arizona Board of Regents
Library of Congress Catalog
Card No. 68-22335
Manufactured in the U.S.A.

CONTENTS

TABLES

MAPS

ACKNOWLEDGMENTS

MANY PEOPLE have been of considerable assistance to me in gathering these data for analysis, putting them into a usable order, and finally presenting the results in a cogent manner.

Tom T. Sasaki provided an invaluable introduction to the field. Robert Cullum of the Bureau of Indian Affairs, Gallup, New Mexico, showed considerable interest in my study during the entire period of field work. My principal Navajo interpreter, Marshall Tome, worked tirelessly at his duties helping me to understand something of Navajo culture and of The People themselves.

David F. Aberle, with considerable wit and enduring patience, stimulated my thinking about the data and their significance. My dissertation committee, consisting of Robert Manners, Helen Codere, and George Cowgill, all of the Department of Anthropology, Brandeis University, also guided the analysis of data and its implications.

My debts are heavy to the Albuquerque Navajos. I hope that this study will not disappoint them. My wife was with me in the field and was a great help in numerous ways. To all of these individuals go my deepest thanks.

I am also grateful to the various publishers and authors who gave me permission to use portions of their writings. Charles Hess prepared the map of the Navajo country and the Department of Anthropology at the University of Wyoming provided financial assistance for the preparation of the map showing the residence distribution of Navajos in Albuquerque. E. W. Jernigan of the University of Arizona drafted the final version of all the maps.

William H. Hodge

University of Wisconsin — Milwaukee
Milwaukee, Wisconsin

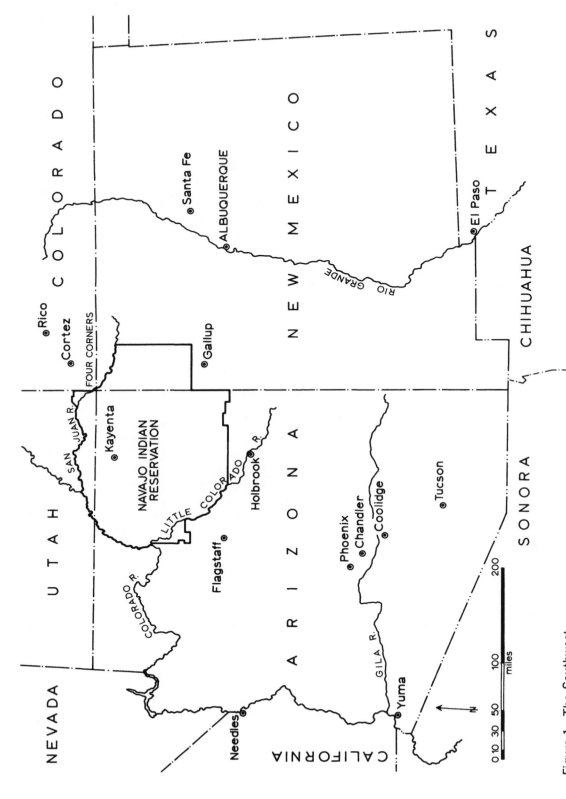

Figure 1. The Southwest

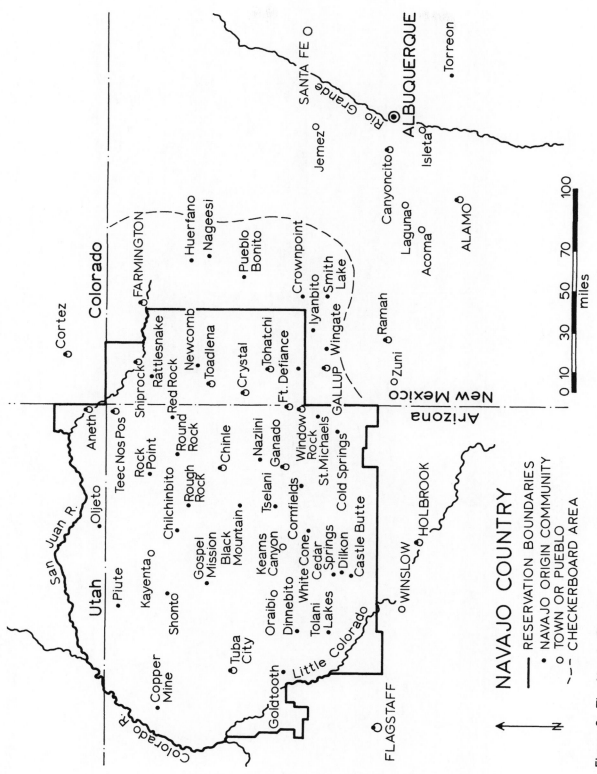

Figure 2. The Navajo Country

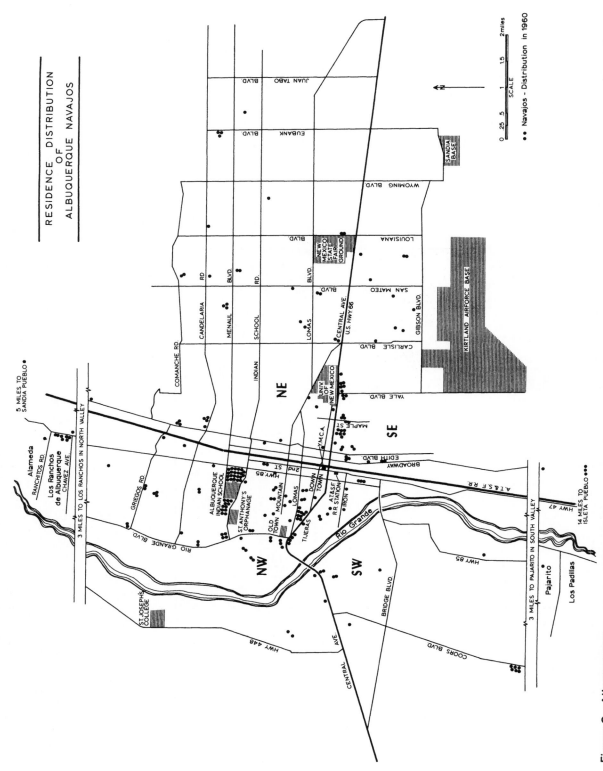

Figure 3. Albuquerque

1. INTRODUCTION

AMERICAN INDIANS have been living in cities for many years. In 1966 there were more than 100,000 of them in the Los Angeles area; 10,000 of this number were Navajo. Chicago had an Indian population of 12,000, the San Francisco Bay area had at least 10,000, and more than 5,000 Indians were working in Denver. In spite of the size of these populations, the general non-Indian population has been almost entirely unaware of them. More surprising is the fact that this lack of awareness for the most part has been shared by social scientists.

Even those social scientists who have known of urban Indians have usually not studied them because of a general lack of interest. Most anthropologists have felt that the proper place to study Indians is on the reservations. Indians living in a city have not been really thought of as Indians any more than Irish or Italian migrants have been viewed as true representations of their European counterparts. Other researchers have felt that most of what can be learned about Indians has been learned. The villages of India and the Caribbean, the African peoples, and the little known inhabitants of Melanesia appear to them to offer more unexploited areas of study.

As a further discouragement, research on urban Indians poses many difficulties. American Indians living in cities are often hard to find, and it is usually difficult to make and maintain adequate contact with them. When this contact can be maintained, it is an arduous task to gather data on a particular problem. If an Indian is to survive in the city, he must work at a job regularly. After working hours he must perform the same necessary tasks that other non-Indian urban residents do. Frequently Indians do not care to share their limited leisure time with an anthropologist. For these and possibly other reasons, American urban Indians have been infrequently studied and comparatively little is known about them.

A 1928 report (Meriam) contains a provocative section on "migrant Indians." However, it was not until twenty-five years after this that a few anthropologists began to recognize that urban Indians could provide suitable material for study. Most of this research has taken the form of M.A. and Ph.D. dissertations written within the last ten years. The present analysis is a part of this developing interest.

This study concerns an aggregate of 275 adult Navajos who were living in Albuquerque, New Mexico, from July, 1959, to June, 1961, the period of my residence there. Research emphasis is given to Navajo men because I found that generally they were not as shy as were Navajo women. Moreover, some Navajo husbands tactfully informed me that they would resent my visiting their wives during the day when they were home alone.

The study attempts to demonstrate why some of the Navajos intended to remain permanently in Albuquerque and why others wanted to return or, in fact, did return to the reservation. The central problem can be phrased thusly: Why are some urban-dwelling Navajos non-permanent residents while others are permanent residents? I define a non-permanent – resident Navajo as one who (a) resides in the city; (b) regards his residence as temporary; and (c) prefers the reservation to the city. A permanent-resident Navajo may be defined as one who (a) resides in the city; (b) has decided to remain in the city; and (c) prefers the city to the reservation.

The answers to the following subsidiary questions should shed light on the central problem: What are those forces which bring a Navajo to Albuquerque, keep him in the city, or pull him back toward the reservation? Once in the city, how does a Navajo earn money to provide himself and his family with food and shelter? How does he live with non-Navajos in an environment which is quite different from the reservation? How does he come to grips with a host of other problems which all urban residents must solve? How do Navajos resemble other Albuquerque Indian and non-Indian residents? How do they differ?

Why do so few Navajos want to stay in Albuquerque? Why do the majority of Navajos want to return to the reservation? How does a formerly urban Navajo want to live if he does return to the reservation?

On the bases of their desire to stay in Albuquerque or to return to the reservation and their general attitudes toward both places, the Navajos can, for purposes of analysis, be placed in three categories according to situation and ideology. The categories are: permanent-resident as defined above, and non-permanent — resident, which can be divided into two sub-categories, *traditional* and *Anglo-modified*. A traditional Navajo speaks little or no English, lives a marginal economic existence in Albuquerque, and wants to return to the reservation as soon as possible to follow a traditional existence there.

The term "Anglo" is used by the general population in the Southwest to refer to a non-Spanish speaking Caucasian. The majority of anthropologists also use this term when writing about Caucasians who live in the Southwest. The term "Anglo-modified Navajo" is regarded as being especially suitable for use here because some Navajos have assumed various characteristics of this Anglo population. An Anglo-modified Navajo would, however, like to return to the reservation as soon as possible and establish residence near or in one of the transitional reservation communities now in existence or in the process of formation: Window Rock, Navajo, Chinle, Kayenta, Tuba City, and others. These transitional communities seem to be regarded by Navajos as service centers where non-traditional employment and western goods and services can be obtained. Here certain selected aspects of traditional Navajo life can hopefully be integrated with various facets of Anglo culture without having to submit to certain unavoidable influences found in Albuquerque which are regarded as undesirable.

The term "Anglo-modified" should not be confused with the standard meaning of the term "marginal" as it has been used by Robert Park and E. C. Hughes. An Anglo-modified Navajo is marginal only in the sense that he desires some of the material goods associated with urban living such as type of housing, sanitary facilities, and certain forms of entertainment. His ethnic identity is not a matter of ambivalence to him. He readily regards himself as a Navajo and is so regarded by other Navajos whether they be traditional, permanent-resident, or

similarly Anglo-modified. By virtue of the fact of long exposure to Anglo ways and extensive training in them, an Anglo-modified Navajo is capable of assuming an Anglo ethnic identity, but he has decided not to do so. It should also be emphasized that the transitional reservation community where an Anglo-modified Navajo hopes to live is not only culturally but geographically distinct from those reservation areas where traditional Navajos are living and urban traditionals hope to live.

HYPOTHESES

A preliminary analysis of the data suggests a number of hypotheses. Part of these have been grouped by the categories defined above.

When one considers what factors determine or are associated with permanent-resident, traditional, or Anglo-modified categories, a complex set of inter-relationships presents itself. Some factors, such as ethnic identity of spouse, spouse's attitude toward reservation life, open or closed reservation background, unpleasant idiosyncratic urban experience, and frequent urban-reservation contacts may operate alone. Other factors have a zero order of correlation when taken by themselves, but together with others seem to be influential, or at least diagnostic of the particular category assumed. Age, education, subsistence forms, military service, presence or absence of a Navajo name, Navajo language ability, and religious orientation are included in this group of factors. Some factors, such as blood, are shared by all three categories and therefore are not of a causal nature.

The various urban areas and the reservations throughout the country can be viewed as urban-reservation systems. To understand fully the significance of Indian urban occupation the modes of Indian reservation living must be considered. For example, Dakota patterns of existence in Rapid City can be fully understood only if the life of Dakotas on the Pine Ridge and Rosebud reservations is simultaneously inspected.

Permanent-Resident Navajos

Many permanent-urban-resident Navajos are such because they were reared in a non-Navajo milieu on the reservation. This "non-Navajo milieu" was the prototype of the present day transitional reservation community which the Anglo-modified Navajo hopes to occupy. Twenty or thirty years ago

Navajo transitional communities consisted of a small number of buildings, a trading post, a Bureau of Indian Affairs (BIA) school together with dormitories and housing for the staff personnel of these units. The trader and the few individuals required for supervisory positions were Anglo. The rest of the community was Navajo.

Communities of this sort (Shiprock, Fort Defiance, and Ganado are examples) were few, and hence a small number of Navajos lived and worked in these communities. The children of these employees were subject to many of the same influences which affected Anglo children off the reservation. Their parents worked five or six days a week for wages and traditional forms of Navajo subsistence were usually not relied upon. Parents hoped that their children would assume an Anglo middle class value system, and the children usually did. Anglo standards of sanitation were viewed as necessary and Anglo education was eagerly sought. Both parents and children regarded traditional Navajo life with indifference or mild contempt.

These Navajos associated with their traditional neighbors, but they generally regarded themselves as superior to them. Once the children had entered an off-reservation boarding school, which was usually around the age of fourteen or fifteen, they seldom returned home. During the summers they worked at various Anglo rural or city jobs. Such a practice was encouraged by the BIA schools. The parents usually regretted their children's absence but felt that off-reservation living was the best thing for them since they really had no place on the reservation. Permanent wage work was scarce on the reservation and a more satisfying life could be found elsewhere.

A Navajo can also become a permanent-urban-resident by the much simpler and more direct process of being born and reared off the reservation or moving away from the reservation permanently at a very young age.

A permanent-resident Navajo will marry a woman who doesn't want to live on the reservation. This hypothesis, however, does not imply that a single person cannot be a permanent resident who has prepared for and has succeeded in obtaining an economic and social urban existence which he regards as satisfactory.

Permanent-resident Navajos are a minority group among Navajos because the influential factors stated in the above hypotheses have affected a comparatively small number of people.

Non-permanent — Resident Navajos

The majority of Albuquerque Navajos are non-permanent urban residents for several reasons. First, they have been reared in a traditional Navajo milieu on the reservation. This traditional milieu has been described in Kluckhohn and Leighton (1946), Leighton and Kluckhohn (1948), and the Franciscan Fathers (1910). Family subsistence is based upon a combination of pastoralism, small-scale dry or irrigated farming, off-reservation seasonal wage work, and some form of relief. The parents have had little or no formal education. Children have had less than a high school education and often no more than one or two years in school. Individuals are enmeshed in a pervasive system of kin rights and obligations.

Other factors contributing to non-permanency are marriage and adjustment. Most non-permanent residents will marry women who do want to live on the reservation. They have not prepared for and have not succeeded in obtaining an economic and social urban existence which is satisfactory to them.

TRADITIONAL NAVAJOS

Indirect but crucial influences cause a large majority of the tribe's members to remain traditional Navajos on the reservation. The industrialization of the Southwest began chiefly with World War II. In many ways, it still lags behind that of the rest of the country. The embryonic state of industrial development on the reservation is a corollary of this fact. Hence, most Navajos still gain their subsistence in the traditional manner. Furthermore, the majority of Navajo children have had access to an educational program comparable to that available to Anglos only within the last five to ten years. Given these conditions, it would seem to follow that most Navajos neither desire nor are prepared for extensive participation in non-reservation life.

A Navajo is traditional because he was reared in a traditional Navajo milieu and had a closed reservation background. A closed reservation background is one which includes few or no Anglo contacts during an individual's formative years. Such a background implies a total absorption in and a total commitment to the traditional way of life.

Such a Navajo marries a Navajo woman who was also reared in a traditional Navajo milieu and had a closed reservation background. His reservation contacts reinforce and maintain his traditional status. If a traditional Navajo works off the reservation at seasonal labor, the majority of his contacts, with the possible exception of his employer, are with other traditional Navajos. If he lives in a city on a temporary basis (and urban residence can only be regarded as temporary for Navajos in this category) his inter-personal relations are also, for the most part, with other traditional Navajos.

For a traditional Navajo, city residence is an accidental situation, usually assumed because of extreme pressures stemming from chronic illness or an impoverished financial situation on the reservation. Many Navajos contract tuberculosis on the reservation and are committed to an urban sanatorium for seven or eight years. Their physicians have suggested that they remain in town for some time after discharge because the possibility of a recurrence of the disease is greater on the reservation than in a city.

Other traditional Navajos are forced to leave the reservation because of the unusually severe poverty of their families and friends. One solution to this situation is for the traditional Navajo to work continuously at "temporary-seasonal" jobs until he acquires enough English and marketable job skills to get a "permanent" job off the reservation, that is, one which he can hold indefinitely provided his job performance is satisfactory. Thus, a traditional Navajo could work in a railroad labor gang until he was laid off and then work a number of vegetable harvests until another railroad job appeared. Eventually, he might be employed as a silversmith in a city or as a laborer on a truck farm near its outskirts, jobs which generally pay more and offer benefits which non-urban seasonal labor does not. However, Navajos in this category return to the reservation as soon as possible to assume permanent residence there.

The lack of formal education and English language skills reinforces this desire to return to a traditional reservation environment, because these lacks automatically block access to many aspects of urban living which are perceived by Navajos to be advantageous. These advantages include additional education of a quality superior to that generally available on the reservation, a variety of forms of recreation, extensive medical facilities, and others.

ANGLO-MODIFIED NAVAJOS

Most Anglo-modified Navajos have had a closed reservation background for the first few years of their lives and have then undergone non-traditional experiences such as boarding school both off and on the reservation.

Many of the Navajos in this category remember their early years on the reservation as unpleasant because they feel that they were taken advantage of by older siblings or parents. They were often forced to remain at home to care for livestock while others in their family went off the reservation for schooling or relatively lucrative seasonal labor. They were given tedious jobs with little or no material reward. Navajos with this sort of background state that they want nothing to do with their kinsmen when they return to the reservation.

An Anglo-modified Navajo's contacts with the reservation while he maintains a residence in the city reinforce his particular orientation. Navajos in this category are subjected to strains in their relationships with the reservation which permanent-resident and traditional Navajos do not experience. Anglo-modified Navajos frequently complain that their rare visits to the reservation are often unpleasant. The family of such a visiting Navajo will expect him to perform the duties he did before going to the city, such as hauling wood and water and herding livestock. The fact that the urban Navajo's visit is usually limited to a weekend does not modify their expectations.

When an Anglo-modified Navajo is visited by his reservation kinsmen, they can be a great source of irritation. They feel that he is immensely wealthy and will not be inconvenienced by an indeterminate visit. Because they frequently cannot speak English, their transportation to and from the reservation is an additional source of inconvenience to him. Instructions have to be given to indifferent bus drivers and the travelers may or may not arrive at their destination at an expected time. Telephones are also a source of trouble. An Anglo-modified Navajo may receive a collect call from the reservation asking for money. A visitor from the reservation will often call friends at home and talk for as long as an hour.

An Anglo-modified Navajo will marry a Navajo spouse with a similar orientation and background or a non-Navajo spouse who is either highly ambivalent regarding reservation living or strongly opposed to it.

Anglo-modified Navajos are drawn toward the

reservation by certain attractions such as the opportunity to use urban-acquired skills to good advantage there. They are also moved to return to the reservation because of unsatisfied job aspirations in the city, and a general dissatisfaction with an urban way of life.

* * *

The fact that urban or reservation residence is desired or adopted has little or nothing to do with ethnic discrimination. Generally it can be said that Navajos come to Albuquerque largely to achieve an optimum level of existence through the utilization of the educational and health facilities and employment opportunities which the city offers.

Navajos survive in Albuquerque because they are able to promote and maintain economic self-reliance. Federal, state, and local welfare aid is not sufficient to support even short-term residence. With the exception of a semi-annual issue of clothing for school children, the tribe provides no support for Albuquerque Navajos. If they go to the reservation, they are eligible for the benefits to which reservation Navajos are entitled, even though they maintain an urban residence. However, since round-trip travel is over 400 miles, few if any of the Albuquerque Navajos use reservation welfare services.

Anglo-modified Navajos stay in Albuquerque either because a desirable niche is not currently available on the reservation or because they have decided that their chances of achieving an optimum level of existence are greatest if temporary urban residence is maintained.

The situation, discussed in terms of the established categories, could be characterized as follows: Traditional Navajos are in Albuquerque because urban residence appears to be the best *temporary* residence choice; Anglo-modified Navajos regard temporary urban residence as better than two other evils — traditional reservation life or permanent urban residence.

It is impossible to determine, and irrelevant for the purposes of this study, whether or not Navajos in the Anglo-modified category realize or admit to themselves that a choice initially regarded as temporary may well become permanent because a niche in a reservation community may never appear. It is probably much harder to find a place in a reservation community than to achieve the goal of the traditional Navajo.

It may be that some Anglo-modified Navajos

enter Albuquerque with the intention of becoming permanent urban residents and never returning to the reservation to live. For one or a number of reasons they have been unable to attain a style of urban living which they view as adequate and necessary. Their aspirations thwarted, or at least beyond immediate reach, they hope to create their own best of all possible worlds by meshing western technology and occupation with reservation residence. However, it might also be that many Anglo-modified Navajos find city life sufficiently unpleasant to take up traditional life on the reservation and wait there for a community vacancy to appear. If one does not develop soon enough, they will again move back to the city and repeat the cycle of unsatisfactory temporary urban residence followed by equally unsatisfactory traditional reservation living.

Permanent-resident Navajos regard themselves only latently as Navajos. For them either type of reservation living, traditional or community, and all that either implies, is hardly possible. For them, urban life does provide a desirable style of life. Urban residence, then, has been willingly and permanently chosen, and is an obvious and necessary choice.

It can be argued that urban Navajo residence is simply another instance of the Navajo tendency — a tendency that has existed for at least 350 years — to take advantage of and rely upon varying resources as they become available while retaining their essential ethnic identity. Following this tendency, some Navajos rely upon the availability of wage labor in an urban setting.

The urban situation is a reflection of the reservation situation insofar as there are traditional and Anglo-modified Navajos in both places. These two categories will persist or disappear together.

Individual economic independence and a heightened level of sophistication regarding non-Navajo society and culture will not necessarily produce middle class Anglo citizens, or individuals who are genetically Navajo but who earnestly wish to emulate Anglo social and cultural forms in an urban setting.

There is, at present, only one way that traditional Navajo and Anglo ways can be successfully combined. This situation can occur when a Navajo becomes a Tribal, Public Health Service (PHS), or BIA employee on the reservation. Virtually all working members of the reservation communities today

6

THE ALBUQUERQUE NAVAJOS

are employed by one of these agencies. Only a very small number of Navajos have their own businesses nor are the reservation activities of private industry numerous.

* * *

It may well be that it is impossible to conclusively prove or disprove all of the hypotheses offered in the preceding pages, but certainly a definite idea can be gained of their order of probability.

The hypotheses given above stem in part from the discussion of D. J. Bogue (1959: 486–509) who provides a useful summary of recent studies of migration within the United States. He regards migration as a process and considers it under a number of topics: (1) Definition; (2) Migration-stimulating situations; (3) Factors in choosing a destination; (4) Socioeconomic conditions affecting migration; (5) Knowledge about migration streams; and (6) Knowledge about differential migration.

SUMMARY

This study concerns an aggregate of 275 adult Navajos who were living in Albuquerque, New Mexico, from July, 1959, to June, 1961, the period of my residence there. Research emphasis is given to Navajo men. The study attempts to demonstrate why some Navajos intended to remain permanently in Albuquerque and why others wanted to return or, in fact, did return to the reservation. A number of hypotheses are offered which guide the study and organize supporting comparative material.

2. COMPARATIVE DATA FOR OFF-RESERVATION INDIANS

To FACILITATE the understanding of data presented in this chapter, efforts made by the federal government toward the promotion of urban relocation have been summarized. This summary should provide a background for the information contained in the ensuing summaries of comparative data.

As was mentioned in Chapter 1, there has been little study devoted to American Indians living away from their reservations in various cities. All published and unpublished material available to me has been carefully read; however, only a small portion of this material is of immediate relevance to this analysis. This pertinent fraction of data is summarized in Table 1. The Navajo sources are treated at greater length in the text.

GOVERNMENT RELOCATION EFFORTS

For more than forty years the Bureau of Indian Affairs and other agencies have been aware that American Indians have serious economic difficulties. Throughout the country, on many Indian reservations and in other areas which have large Indian populations, opportunities for self-support are lacking because land resources are insufficient in either quantity or quality and industrial development is negligible. Hence, many Indians must either leave their birthplaces to seek new opportunities or remain on the reservations, living in privation or depending either wholly or partially on some form of public assistance. Madigan (1956: 3) quotes a letter from

TABLE 1

LOCATION OF URBAN INDIANS
OTHER THAN NAVAJO

City	Tribe	Reference	City	Tribe	Reference
New York City	Mohawk	Freilich 1958, Mitchell 1949	San Francisco Bay Area (Oakland, San Jose, San Francisco)	Eskimo, Haida, Tsimshian, Tlingit, Kiowa, Sioux, Pomo	Hirabayashi 1964
St. Louis	Sioux, Sac and Fox, Ponca	Verdet 1961		Sioux, Turtle Mountain Chippewa, Laguna, Acoma	Ablon 1964
Chicago	Sioux, Chippewa Menomini	Verdet 1961 Slotkin 1957		Crow, Northern Cheyenne	Hanson 1960
Milwaukee	Oneida, Stockbridge, Chippewa, Winnebago, and Brotherton	Meriam 1928	Portland	Klamath, Chippewa	Ebihara and Kelley 1955
	Oneida, Stockbridge, Chippewa, Menomini, Winnebago, Potawatomi	Ritzenthaler and Sellers 1955	Dallas	Sioux, Choctaw	Martin 1964
			Los Angeles	Mission, Papago, Pima	Meriam 1928
Minneapolis-St. Paul	Chippewa Dakota Sioux,	Mann 1957	Needles, Kingman, Globe, and Miami	Apache, Mohave, Walapai	Meriam 1928
	Winnebago, Chippewa	Manzolillo 1955	Yuma	Yuma	Bee 1963
			Phoenix	Hopi, Apache, Papago, Pima, Maricopa	Meriam 1928
Rapid City	Dakota Sioux	Carter 1953, Lovrich 1952, Frantz 1953, White 1962, Macgregor 1946	Tucson	Yaqui Papago Papago, Sobaipuris	Spicer 1940, 1962 Spicer 1962 Getty 1950
Yankton	Dakota Sioux	Hurt 1960, 1961-62	Winslow, Flagstaff	Hopi, Laguna Hopi	Meriam 1928 McPhee 1953
Sioux City	Winnebago, Dakota Sioux	Meriam 1928	Santa Fe	Eastern Pueblos	Meriam 1928

Commissioner of Indian Affairs Emmons which states:

We must face facts and one of the most important facts is that there is a definite physical limit to resource development on the reservations. The Navajo Reservation in Arizona, New Mexico and Utah is a good illustration. Under the most optimistic estimate the resources of this reservation, after full development, might be expected to provide a decent livelihood for about 45,000 people. Yet the present Navajo population is about 78,000 and, if present growth trends continue, the population will reach 100,000 by 1962 and approximately 350,000 by the year 2000.

The *Employment Security Review* (1959: 27) notes that in 1930 the Bureau of Indian Affairs initiated a program to obtain off-reservation employment for Indians. Those who benefited most from this effort were recent graduates from the various Bureau-operated schools. Some migration from the reservations by young people was stimulated by this effort, but the depression of the 1930's and federal work relief projects which provided subsistence income at home negated most of its influence. The program was abandoned in 1940.

Relocation efforts began again in 1949 (Cullum 1957: 5) with the off-reservation placement of Indians without financial assistance. In the spring of 1952 Bureau assistance was made available. This practice is continuing at the present time.

The relocation process is administered by BIA offices on or near the reservations and by those located in the several relocation cities. Field Relocation Offices are situated in eight cities: Los Angeles, San Francisco, Oakland, San Jose, Denver, Dallas, Chicago, and Cleveland. The Minneapolis-St. Paul area and St. Louis formerly had offices, but they have recently been discontinued. Under the regulations of the relocation program, Indians may be given financial assistance in moving from reservations only if they select one of these eight cities as a destination.

Madigan (1956: 6–7) provides a good summary of the formal relocation procedure. Essentially, this procedure constitutes a "careful" screening of applicants on the reservation by Bureau officials, an informal but adequate training of accepted applicants for urban life before they reach the city, and a careful supervision of their activities during the first year of their urban residence.

Amounts of money authorized to be given to relocatees in 1956 seemed small, varying from a maximum amount per week of $40 for a husband and wife without children for a maximum period of four weeks to a maximum amount of $100 per week for a man, wife, and eight or more children for a maximum period of four weeks. In addition to this standard scale of allotments, a city Relocation Officer could authorize up to three weeks' emergency subsistence to relocatees who had lost their employment through no fault of their own and were not yet eligible for unemployment compensation.

The *Navajo Times* (Aug. 22, 1963: 4) reported that the amount of financial assistance had been increased, but even then little more than a marginal existence was provided for. The next payment scale ranged from $200 "maximum finance" for a single individual to $895 for a family head and nine or more dependents. The *Times* implied that these amounts were awarded only in cases of extreme hardship.

Bureau assistance in connection with relocation is normally granted only once. Participation in the program is voluntary. Cullum (1957: 1) characterizes the objectives of the relocation program:

The objectives of the Navajo Agency (and all other agencies as well) are to assist Navajo people to become self-supporting on a standard of living conducive to economic security and to become a part of the economic and social life of the nation.

The extent to which the various facets of the formal relocation program are actually implemented is problematical. It is reasonable to assume that many more Indians have moved to cities without federal aid than with it. However, much of the data used by students studying urban Indians is concerned with relocatees, and thus the urban residents best known have been subjected, in one way or another, to the relocation program.

Closely allied to relocation and often complementary to it is the Adult Vocational Training Program. Young (1961: 324) states that in an effort to overcome the obstacles posed by the lack of useful vocational skills on the part of individuals otherwise capable of entering industrial employment, the Bureau widened the scope of its services after November, 1957, to encompass an adult vocational training program. A variety of training courses are available in the various relocation cities and in a few cities not having relocation offices such as Albuquerque. Available courses include training in industrial and building skills, office work, personal service, auto mechanics, engineering, drafting, commercial art, gardening, floristry, and landscaping. The Branch of Relocation Services pays the cost of transportation to the training location and the living expenses of trainees during the training period, which does not exceed two years. When their education is completed, graduates are assisted in finding employment. Since some may receive their training in cities located near their reservation where jobs may not be readily available, they may be encouraged to resettle where there is a demand for their particular skills.

Based upon a generally favorable work experience during World War II, a program was established in 1955 for the regular recruitment of Navajos as section workers on the Union Pacific Railroad. This service seemed to have an appeal for non-English-speaking Indians who were unfamiliar with life off the reservation for more than short periods of time. However, the relocation experience of the majority of workers was not satisfactory, and the program was dropped after two years. Cullum (1957: 20) regards its influence on the tribe as slight.

A statement released by the BIA and published by the *Navajo Times* (Dec. 19, 1963: 17) provides a recent assessment of the relocation program. Self-financed Indian urban migrants are also mentioned:

During the past twelve fiscal years, 1952 through 1963, nearly 30,000 Indian workers have received employment assistance. Of these, some 17,000 or 60 per cent have become permanently employed. With their families, they total 36,000 persons. This total includes nearly 26,000 persons who have been benefited from direct relocation to employment that has proved permanent. It includes nearly 9,000 others, for a total of about 35,000 who have been enabled by Bureau training to effect such relocation. It includes more than 1,000 for whom on-the-job training had led to employment on or near the reservations. It does not include other thousands who, motivated by the example of their friends and relatives under the Bureau program, have successfully left the reservation or have found jobs nearby without benefit of any aspect of the Bureau program. How many thousands should be added to the 35,000 "relocatees" accounted for under the Bureau program it is not possible to say with accuracy. At the present time, the program is operating at a level that may be expected to enable more than 2500 workers (over 6,000 family members) a year to complete successful transfer to the outside American society....

Those who successfully complete the program and become part of the off-reservation labor force do so on the average only with their third job. With the Bureau's assistance in finding the right job, however, and with continued assistance, which is required by about 10 per cent of these workers, unemployment seems to be kept well below the average. Our most recent examination of this was in 1958. It was found that unemployment among resettled Indian workers during the 1957-58 recession averaged less than 4 per cent, as compared with a national average of over 7 per cent....

Only about one-third of relocated Indian workers are family men. We are confident, however, that the job qualifications and stable work habits acquired by all who succeed in establishing themselves off the reservation under the program is such as to sustain their performance above the national average and similarly to hold their unemployment rate below the U.S. norm....

The Indians who have successfully relocated away from the reservations in recent years are, of course, not typical of all members of the non-reservation population. They do constitute a full 20 per cent or more of the non-reservation population, however, of which another 50 per cent or more are children or grandchildren of Indians who succeeded a generation or more ago in making their way in the outside world. Many of these are included by the Census in the Indian population solely on the basis of their own ethnic self-identification. Such Indians as these are members of a minority group only in the same sense that those of Scotch-Irish ancestry are a minority in the country. The balance of the non-reservation population, perhaps a fifth, includes many Indians who are far from fully absorbed into the general American population. Among such we must expect high rates of economic deprivation and of unemployment similar to those among unassimilated Puerto Ricans and other recent arrivals.

Relocation, of course, is not regarded by the government as a universal panacea for the economic plight of the Indian. Improvement is also sought in reservation industrial development and other measures.

SYNOPSIS OF COMPARATIVE DATA

The Navajo residents of Albuquerque are not considered in this section. Data regarding other off-reservation Navajos are divided into two general categories: those concerning seasonal or temporary residence and those concerning permanent residence. Where the quantity of data warrants, permanent off-reservation residence will be discussed both chronologically and by urban area.

Temporary Off-reservation Residents

T. T. Sasaki (1960: 45–6) provides data regarding an early instance of off-reservation Navajo employment. His comments apply to Navajos living near Fruitland, New Mexico, for whom wage work opportunities away from the reservation were present beginning in the early 1880's. The building of the Denver and Rio Grande railroad tracks in this vicinity was a source of work which many Navajos readily utilized. A few of the area's Indians went as far as Kansas and Oklahoma for farm employment.

The first long period of wage labor for the majority of Fruitland Navajo men, however, was provided by the Work Projects Administration and the Civilian Conservation Corps in the 1930's. Most men had off-reservation jobs during World War II, and since 1945 the majority have left for off-reservation employment immediately after their work in the fields is completed. Most Navajos work for the large corporation farms that have been established at Bluewater, New Mexico; Cortez and Fort Lewis, Colorado; and Phoenix, Arizona. Others work for the railroads as section hands without their families, and a smaller portion are hired by a few Colorado mines. Occasionally, the few Navajo stone masons and carpenters earn money in nearby reservation border towns.

Spicer (1962: 556–7) discusses temporary and permanent off-reservation employment and its implications for the Navajos as a whole. Navajos did not seek work off the reservation in any numbers until after 1910 when an increasing population density there made the raising of livestock and farming more difficult than it had been prior to this time. A large demand for Navajo labor did not appear until the 1940's. By 1956 the railroads were employing about 6,500 Navajos a year in part-time unskilled jobs. Smaller numbers had been hired by various light industries along the southern edge of the reservation and in the larger cities such as Albuquerque, Phoenix, Tucson, and El Paso.

During the 1950's, however, most Navajos retained permanent residence on the reservation and many families derived some support from flocks of sheep and limited small-scale farming. The largest part of subsistence for the majority of families came from wages earned by some member of the extended family who worked from three to eight months a year off the reservation. Family heads and unmarried young men left their kinsmen at home and worked either singly or in groups. The money earned by this activity was spent at the local trading post for the purchase of Anglo food stuffs and other merchandise. Such things as pick-up trucks were also purchased in various reservation border towns. These economic adjustments stimulated several kinds of cultural change. In the early part of this decade an extensive federal construction program devoted to schools and roads provided reservation wage work for many Navajos, and even induced a few off-reservation urban residents to return home. This

was an economic adjustment similar to that which had occurred on most of the reservations during the early 1930's.

Kluckhohn (1946: 111–2) makes a number of general observations regarding temporary off-reservation workers. Along with Spicer he notes that population growth is forcing an increasing number of Navajos into economic competition with Anglos, chiefly as unskilled workers. In his relations with an Anglo employer, the Navajo is passive and content to occupy a subordinate position. Kluckhohn's book further states:

It is the writer's impression that many Navajos who seek wage work with whites in nonwar years tend to be those who, for one reason or another, do not get along in their own society. Such maladjusted persons are of course likely to be unstable. But almost all Navajos feel so out of place, so uneasy, in a white environment that they can stand it for just so long. . . . With a few days or weeks at home, attending ceremonials and renewing the sense of participation in the cooperative activities of their familial society, they feel sufficiently relieved and restored to go back to their jobs. But the job to them is a way of earning necessary money, not a way of life.

Kluckhohn argues that there are two chief factors which hinder a Navajo's absorption into the Anglo world: the language barrier and the Navajo's inability to understand the rules for competing with non-Navajos. He feels that these obstacles can be surmounted only by prolonged experience.

W. Y. Adams (1963: 129–35) describes seasonal off-reservation work for the community of Shonto. In 1955 the combination of wages and unemployment compensation from railroad work accounted for more than half the community's total income. Railroad wages mean the difference between bare subsistence and a comfortable material standard of living. At Shonto, for the most part, railroad work for Navajos consists of maintenance of track and work in seasonal extra gangs on the Atchison, Topeka, and Santa Fe Railway. Extra gangs are used as they are needed, which is normally every year during the summer months.

Railroad work appeals to Shonto men because of its associated unemployment compensation. A worker who has earned more than $400 during any calendar year is entitled to compensation for every day of unemployment, which is usually $3.50 to $8.50 per day depending upon his wages during the past fiscal year. Total compensation is limited to an amount equal to twice the previous year's wages. A man becomes eligible for compensation if he formally expresses a desire to work and finds that work is unavailable. Since the local trader acts as a labor recruiter for the Railway and administers unemployment payments, few, if any, Navajos will receive unemployment compensation if they reject work opportunities. The trader is interested in an efficient recruiting program because most Railway wages are spent at his store. Further, unemployment payments seldom equal the previous year's wages because of current employment opportunities.

Generally eligibility for unemployment benefits usually opens up in October or November. Not more than a fraction of Shonto's claim load is likely to be eligible initially, as some workers are still on the road and many others will have returned voluntarily. . . . The claim load mounts rapidly in November and December. Usually all or nearly all claimants are drawing compensation by the first of the new year, and continue to do so until around the first of April (Adams 1963: 133).

Adams found that other forms of outside wage work played a small and unimportant part in Shonto's economy, largely because non-railroad·work does not fit into the traditional seasonal pattern. In an emergency, when nothing else is available, a few people will work at harvesting crops or in defense plants for a few weeks or months, then return to the community. Despite regular recruiting programs by the Arizona State Employment Service, the people of Shonto do not do harvest work because of unsatisfactory working conditions and low pay.

Ebihara and Kelley (1955: 12–3) offer some data on Navajo railroad workers in Portland. At the time of their study between seventy-five and eighty men plus two women and five children were in the area. They had little to do with other Indians and Anglos. The social contacts of these Navajos were limited strictly to other Navajos; indeed, they seemed to associate almost exclusively with those Navajos who happened to be working on the same gang. These Indians lived in modified freight cars in the northeast part of town. Their employer, the Union Pacific Railroad, required them to sign ninety-day contracts and gave them the option of renewing them for an equal time period or returning to the reservation. The Navajos stated that they preferred to remain off the reservation in labor gangs rather than return to the marginal economic conditions of the reservation.

Little is known about leisure time Navajo activities when they are engaged in this seasonal

labor. Available data may well give a distorted impression.

The *Christian Indian* (Dec. 1962: 7) reported that three Navajo railroad laborers along with twenty-seven other Indians were arrested in a raid on a peyote meeting near Needles, California.

The *Navajo Times* (Feb. 4, 1965: 9) stated that about 450 Navajos were working currently in Yuma and Maricopa Counties in Arizona as replacements for Mexican braceros. Over 360 were harvesting lettuce in Yuma, at a minimum wage of $1.05 per hour or better. The harvesting of melons, celery, carrots, cabbage, dry onions, and potatoes supposedly would provide work through the coming summer. The *Times* notes:

Growers and other observers in the Yuma area report that these people are very quick to learn the job, have excellent manual dexterity, and are willing workers.

The next issue of the *Times* (Feb. 11, 1965: 1–8) quoted the *Yuma Daily Sun* (Jan. 19, 1965) as stating that out of 167 Navajos working in the fields near Yuma 50 had quit, 27 were missing, and the remainder had been put in the Yuma County Jail for drunkenness. The total arrests were estimated at more than 80. The *Times* said that the Yuma paper was exaggerating the Navajos' misconduct. It then stated that an investigating committee from the Tribe discovered the actual situation to be as follows: On January 21, a total of 46 Navajos had been booked for disorderly conduct. Since that date, 27 more had been jailed. The Navajo workers complained of poor food and housing and of the fact that a bootlegger was selling whiskey at $2.00 a quart in the camp.

Permanent Off-reservation Residents

THE BAY AREA:
OAKLAND – SAN JOSE – SAN FRANCISCO

Kroeber (1961: 157) mentions that a Navajo was employed in a curio shop in San Francisco in 1908. From this date to 1953, I have no information regarding Navajo residents. Cullum (1957: 7) states that during the fiscal years 1953–56 inclusive, 125 Navajos came to the Bay Area under the relocation program. Ninety-two of these came in family groups. Thirty single men and three single women came. By the end of fiscal year 1956, fifty people or 40 per cent of the total had returned to the reservation. Most of the Navajos coming to the area during this time found semi-skilled or skilled work in factories.

During the period 1955–56, a Navajo Club was formed which had about 25 members who worked at skilled and professional occupations. None of these individuals came to the area *via* the relocation program.

Data on Navajos in the Bay Area are fragmentary, and provide only a vague idea of urban Navajo activity. What material is available is presented in chronological order.

The *Navajo Times* (Sept. 20, 1960: 4) reported that the tribal relocation committee had visited the Bay Area and made this flaccid statement:

The Relocation Services Committee enjoys its work because it feels that its work is worthwhile. And our fellow Navajos in the cities who, with few exceptions, never look to the Tribe for any kind of help because they are making their way, never fail to tell us to carry back the word to our Tribal Chairman and to you Council members that they appreciate having this Committee come to visit them.

Joan Ablon (1964: 298–9) worked in this area during the period 1961–63, and comments that Navajos tend to associate almost exclusively with other Navajos of their own age group who are relatives. Some friendships grow out of common housing and participation in formal group events. She feels that Navajos are more restricted socially than other Indians because of their poor grasp of English, limited exposure to formal schooling, and inherent shyness. A Navajo Club was formed in Oakland, but not more than a dozen people attended meetings. Factionalism was already a serious problem. Most of the area's Navajos appeared to have no interest in formal activity, whether the activity was Navajo, pan-Indian, or Anglo.

The *Navajo Times* (Apr. 18, 1962: 5) states that there were over 700 Navajos in the Oakland area. The tribal relocation committee reported that they were impressed by "the very nice homes which they have purchased and the way they have adapted to the new surroundings." This same source (Sept. 5, 1962: A9) stated that there were no Indian "ghetto situations," since Navajos have spread throughout the community in all types of jobs. The committee chairman, Hoska Cronemeyer, said that there could be no pan-Indian housing districts because "the cultural differences between tribes and members of tribes are too great." The committee was optimistic about the integration of Navajos into the community. This area has one of the lowest reservation-return rates in the country. The Oakland Relocation Office gets twenty to twenty-five new applications a month for both family and individual relocation or schooling.

The *Times* (Aug. 15, 1963: 1, 15, 20) reported on another relocation committee survey of the area. The committee found that many Navajos lacked adequate training for well-paying jobs. There was frequent changing of jobs which compounded adjustment difficulties. Effective communication between relocatees, the BIA, and the Tribe was lacking. Later the *Times* (Sept. 5, 1963: B11–12) quoted the committee's report to the effect that most Bay Area Navajos were satisfied with it as a place to live and were adjusting in a satisfactory manner. However, a number of valid complaints were made regarding the procedures of the BIA relocation facilities: It is a mistake to send large families to Bay Area cities because of the housing expense and the difficulty of finding suitable housing; periods of off-season employment should be considered in sending new relocatees because many of the people already in the area lose their jobs during these periods and need priority consideration for employment in a "tight labor market"; there is a critical shortage of emergency funds at the local BIA Field Offices. Most individuals questioned resented the fact that they were not getting the same welfare services provided to resident Navajos on the reservation.

LOS ANGELES

The 1928 report (Meriam 727) states that there were Navajos living in Los Angeles in the 1920's, but provides no further information. Cullum (1957: 7) reports that for the fiscal years 1953–56, 705 Navajos came to Los Angeles under the relocation program. The great majority of these people came as families. By the end of fiscal year 1956, about 40 per cent of the Navajos had returned to the reservation. The *Navajo Times* (Apr. 18, 1962: 5) estimated that there were over 2,500 Navajos in the Los Angeles area.

A more recent issue (Sept. 17, 1964: 8, 22) gives an account of the local Navajo Club. The club was formed by a number of Navajos aided by an Anglo clergyman in the early 1950's to "help themselves and other Navajos adjust to this new, sometimes frightening, always lonesome, huge, alien monster known as L.A." A few years later, because of factionalism stimulated by rival church groups, the club became independent of Anglo sponsorship, but its

... policies and objectives remained very much the same only with a more deliberate emphasis on Navajo culture, the club serving as an effective public relations and educational group in furthering [Anglo] understanding of the Navajo and the difference in the Navajo and other tribes, their religion, art, dress, foods, dances and ceremonials as distinguished from the Hollywood influenced plains dances and culture which has been for years the main picture of the American Indian in Los Angeles and probably throughout much of the country beyond the bounds of the Southwest or immediate environs of other Indian groups. . . . (8)

Then, too, Navajos lost in an alien culture began to feel a greater appreciation of and pride in their heritage, as (Anglos) began to question them about their people, language, arts, religion, etc., they found that this was something of priceless value which back on the reservation they had taken for granted or at school or church had been taught to look down upon. So [stimulated by Anglo interest] . . . they realized that Navajo identity as a culture need not be lost to the white man's way or overshadowed by the brilliant display of the plains war dance. (8)

The club supposedly helps Navajos who are having financial and/or emotional difficulties in the city. This article supplies a number of other facts: Installation of club officers is "carried on with dignity and in Navajo dress" (22); Los Angeles Navajos hold a variety of jobs, ranging from unskilled labor to engineering. Some live very well materially and others do not.

The article concludes:

How long the Navajo Club will survive or any other group formed in the same spirit will survive will depend upon either the need for social aid or the pride in being Navajo or as in the past the combination. One hopes that while the years bring ever increasing social adjustment that they will not lessen the sense of pride in being Navajo. (22)

BARSTOW, CALIFORNIA

Navajos, according to Cullum (1957: 3) have lived in this small community for at least thirty-five years, working either for the Santa Fe or Union Pacific Railroad or the Marine Supply Center. In 1962, over 300 Navajos were here. A Navajo Club has been formed and some Navajos take part in local church activities and sporting events. Navajo residents are eligible for some tribal welfare benefits such as clothing for school children.

DENVER

Cullum (1957: 7) says that for the fiscal years 1953-56 forty-eight Navajos came to Denver under the relocation program. Twenty-seven went there as families. Eight people or 13 per cent returned to the reservation by the end of fiscal year 1956.

DALLAS

Martin (1964: 290–5) has examined the relationship between selected characteristics of relocated Indians and their behavioral adjustment while on relocation. Adjustment was conceived as ranging from good — an individual who is "highly motivated and indicates no serious problems" — to poor — one who has "poor motivation, job performance," and so forth (p. 295).

During the period September, 1957, to July, 1961, 1,348 individuals and families from 79 different tribes relocated in Dallas (p. 291). The Navajo, Sioux, and Choctaw tribes accounted for about 43 per cent of the total, and 311 cases were selected from these tribes for study. Martin finds that Navajos have "displayed adaptive-like behavior more frequently" than have the Choctaw and Sioux. Such variables as formal education and military experience seem to have an indeterminate correlation with the kind of urban adjustment made.

The *Navajo Times* (Nov. 28, 1963: 4) provides more recent data regarding Navajos in Dallas:

There are presently some 300 Navajo single and family units presently working or attending technical, vocational and business schools in this area under the Bureau of Indian Affairs' Employment Assistance program.

The article includes some excerpts from the report of the Tribe's relocation committee chairman, Raymond Smith:

. . . larger families had more difficulty getting by in terms of wages and housing . . . people in the large families have less schooling and therefore can get only laborer jobs at lower pay . . . . many health problems of relocated Navajo people could be reduced or eliminated by closer physical examinations on the reservation . . . . emergency funds held by the field offices should be increased and cooperation increased with other [federal] agencies. A Navajo speaking employee was recommended for placement in the Dallas office . . . . communications between relocatees and the field office should be improved . . . . the Dallas-Fort Worth Navajo people feel that their children should also be entitled to the benefits of the school children's clothing program as these people say that their take home income after rent does not allow sufficient funds for buying good clothes such as the other children wear. . . . [There is a problem involved] in sending families with a little grasp of English on the part of the husband and none on the part of the wife on relocation. . . . These people should be discouraged from leaving the reservation.

Smith said that the visiting tribal delegation to Dallas experienced the same orientation given a relocated family arriving in the city, which included:

. . . how to ride a bus and to make change for bus fare, how to get a job, how to live in an apartment, how to shop in a supermarket, how to enroll the children in school, how to budget money and many other practical aspects of city living. . . . [Smith] "Not knowing much about these things in a city before, I learned what it was about. If the lecture could have been given in the Navajo language, I probably would have understood it better."

CHICAGO

During the fiscal years 1953–56 Cullum (1957: 7) reports that 94 Navajos came to Chicago under the relocation program. By the end of the fiscal year 1956, 42 people had returned to the reservation. As in the case of Denver, Los Angeles, and the Bay Area most Navajos came as families.

The *Navajo Times* during the period 1960–64 reported on ten large families which had come to Chicago. In spite of inadequate vocational training and serious financial difficulties, the *Times* said that they would be content to remain, at least for the time being, in this city.

The *Times* during this same period also stated that the cities of Chicago, Cleveland, and Dallas were especially good places to relocate because of persistent employment opportunities.

The *Times* (Nov. 5, 1964: 1, 10) commented on a Navajo who was working at an Amarillo TV station as a professional Indian. Fred Johnson or "Chief Proud Eagle" had his own children's show. Johnson formerly worked at a radio station in Farmington.

Reservation Border Town Residents

A single source (McPhee: 1953) provides most of the data for this section. The data were collected during 1951. Much of the data is presented in terms of Navajo *and* Hopi activity. Where it is impossible to determine which tribe is being referred to, the term "Navajo-Hopi" is used.

WINSLOW, ARIZONA

A total of 68 families, 33 Navajo (148 individuals) and 35 Hopi (197 individuals), were interviewed. It is estimated that at least 80 per cent of the resident Indian families were contacted. Forty out of the 68 Navajo-Hopi families (59 per cent) interviewed had been living in Winslow for four years or more.

Fifteen (22 per cent) had lived there less than one year. Of these 15, 12 families were working at seasonal jobs and were in the habit of returning to Winslow from the reservation for periods of from three to seven months. The report concludes that the Indian population of Winslow is fairly stable.

Indian housing was rated as "adequate." Thirteen families were living in a squatter's camp near the edge of town. When a family left this camp, it dismantled its two-room shack dwelling and carried the material with it. Two privy toilets served the entire camp. Garbage was usually thrown in a pit. Sanitary standards seemed to be no worse than those existing at the more crowded converted tourist courts where some Indians lived. Most of the Indians at the camp had been living there from three to ten years. Forty-five Navajo-Hopi families lived in rented houses in town. There was some discrimination shown toward Indians in the matter of housing.

Most Indian children attended local public schools. The majority of Indian residents were satisfied with Winslow law enforcement agencies. Public welfare facilities were seldom used because most Navajo-Hopi families returned to their reservations when in trouble.

Indians in Winslow were largely unaware of and had not been invited into local civic or recreational groups, with the exception of some school and church functions.

HOLBROOK, ARIZONA

In 1951, Holbrook had a population of 2,300. About 200 (8 per cent) of the residents were Indians. The 131 Indians interviewed estimated that the 35 Navajo-Hopi families and single adults contacted comprised more than 80 per cent of the residents from these two tribes.

The economy of Holbrook centered around the Santa Fe Railway, ranching, and the tourist trade. Most of those contacted worked for the railroad or on construction. The majority of the Indians worked at semi-skilled and unskilled jobs. Over half of the Navajo-Hopi had been in town for less than a year. Most had less than an elementary education. Housing and general sanitary conditions appeared to be adequate. The Indian population seldom used such community facilities as credit, banking, church services, and welfare agencies. Apparently very few children attended the public schools. No data are given regarding discrimination.

FLAGSTAFF AND BELLEMONT, ARIZONA

In 1950 Flagstaff had a population of 7,663. The survey revealed that 5,000 people lived in a shabby area south of the Santa Fe Railway tracks. Bellemont is an Army post located ten miles west of Flagstaff. A large proportion of the civilian personnel consisted of Navajo and Hopi Indians, who lived in a camp near the military installation.

In Flagstaff a total of 81 families, 51 Navajo with 223 individuals were interviewed. In and near Bellemont a total of 149 families, 131 Navajo with 700 individuals, and 18 Hopi with 98 individuals were interviewed. No accurate information concerning the number of Navajo and Hopi families living in Flagstaff could be obtained, but estimates varied from 50 to 100. It is probable that at least 80 per cent of the families were interviewed (McPhee 1953: 35).

A number of general observations can be gleaned from this portion of the report. Most of the Indians living at Flagstaff and Bellemont were permanent residents who had been in the area for more than two years. Indians were satisfactory workers. Indian housing compared favorably with non-Indian dwellings. Most Indian children attended public schools, but very few Indians participated in community life. Members of the transient Indian population were frequently in trouble with the local police because of drunken behavior. Most of the area's Indians maintained close ties with their reservations. There may have been strong anti-Indian feelings in the community.

GALLUP, NEW MEXICO

For present purposes, the Gallup area consists of the city of Gallup, Wingate Village, and the small settlement at Perea, east of Gallup. In McPhee's survey 402 Navajo families were contacted, a number which was estimated to be 85 to 90 per cent of the resident Navajo population. The report provides the following useful summary:

The population is composed of a group of families which, on an average, are smaller in size than a cross section of reservation families. The average number of persons per family residing in Gallup was 4.5 while a study made of a group of reservation families in this work area revealed an average of 6.5 persons per family in a representative group. Contributing factors seemed to be the greater percentage of single or widowed heads of families and an absence of dependent adult relatives in the homes (McPhee 1953: 12).

In addition, McPhee concludes that Navajos lived in Gallup because they could find work there.

About 15 per cent of the Gallup Navajos retained homes on the reservation and attempted to maintain kin ties and obligations there. Those contacted stated that there was no discrimination toward the Navajo by local residents and that the community generally constituted a good place to work and live. However, all Navajos felt that there was a critical shortage of good housing available at prices which they could afford.

McPhee (1953: 4) states that the Wingate Ordnance Depot employed 190 Navajos, followed by the BIA with 47, and private construction contractors with 34. Thirty-three Navajos worked as full-time silversmiths, and 84 women were employed as domestics. Out of the 190 employees at Wingate, 143 were laborers.

A number of miscellaneous but pertinent observations were made concerning Gallup Navajos: About half of them owned cars or trucks. Seventy-seven per cent rented their homes. Only 15 per cent of those contacted said that they visited friends and relatives on the reservation frequently. The remainder either seldom visited the reservation or spent all of their leisure time in town.

Gallup Navajos expressed no interest in local civic groups. About half the Navajo residents had used some public relief. There were only nineteen Navajos who had a non-Navajo spouse and four of this number were married to non-Indians. Many Navajos had trouble with liquor, but the majority of these were not permanent residents. Several church and secular groups sponsored welfare and social centers for Navajos. The extent of participation in these organizations by Gallup Navajos is unknown.

In 1960, Gallup had a population of about 14,000. The State Employment Security Commission (Zickefoose 1962: 3) estimated that at least 5,500 Indians fourteen years of age or older lived in the area. Some of these were Laguna, Zuni, and Hopi; the remainder were Navajo. Sears (1954: 4) states that at least 31 per cent of the county's total retail sales were made to Indians. Zickefoose (1962: 3) says that the economic development associated with World War II and the post-war development of nearby uranium resources contributed to an increase of 470 per cent in the per capita income of the Navajos from 1940 to 1958.

FARMINGTON, NEW MEXICO

In 1950, Farmington had a population of 3,637. In

the report compiled by McPhee, 59 Navajo families were interviewed, including 106 adult Navajos who were established residents of the town or who had recently secured employment there and planned to remain permanently in the community (1953: 14). The 59 families had a total of 145 children, and 73 of these were of school age.

For the sake of brevity, the relevant data for the most part can be presented in a series of abbreviated statements. All adult Navajos spoke Navajo, and 86 also spoke English. Twelve families spoke little or no English. About half had completed no more than six years of school, but most parents encouraged their children to attend local public schools. About one-third of the men worked as laborers, while the rest had semi-skilled and skilled jobs. Most Navajos had been in Farmington for no more than two years. They liked living in Farmington, and, although they seldom participated in civic activities, they felt that Navajo residents were well adjusted. Resident Navajos were law-abiding; the large number of Navajos arrested for drunkenness in Farmington were living on the reservation.

As is the case with most of the border towns, Farmington had a shortage of adequate housing, and sanitary facilities were of poor quality. Twenty-three Navajo families were living in tents. Two families had residences in Farmington and on the reservation.

Parker (1954) provides some useful supplementary data on Farmington and its Navajo residents which in many respects contradicts the 1953 McPhee study. During the period 1950 to 1954 the population increased from 3,637 to 12,000. This rapid growth stemmed, for the most part, from the exploitation of the extensive natural gas resources in the area. Wholesale and retail trade outlets expanded correspondingly.

By 1954, there were about 80 permanent Navajo households in Farmington. Parker (1954: 7) characterizes the settlement pattern and general living conditions.

For the most part the Navajo population in town resides in two separate areas. One is on the extreme eastern end of the town and the other on the western outskirts. About three quarters of the families inhabit the former pocket which is often referred to as "Tent City." This concentration of Navajos consists of closely packed tents on the bank of the Animas River. Since there is no city water available, most of the families obtain drinking water from water hydrants located nearby. However, many still use water from the river for various purposes. The sanitation problem is rather acute since there are no sanitary facilities available in Tent City. Individuals usually relieve themselves in a bush near the river. Some families have constructed outdoor privies. . . . A few Navajo families live in brick or wooden frame houses in the residential district of the town.

Most of the tents were in poor condition and the "frame houses" were small one-room shacks of poor construction. Parker feels that some of the problems the Navajos face in trying to adjust to town life stem from their poor housing.

The principal employer of Navajos in the area, the El Paso Natural Gas Company, stated that it had trouble with the Indians. Much of the difficulty stemmed from the poor command of English by the Navajos. Also, Navajos wanted to work only with other Navajos. They resented being switched from one task to another. They did not want to "advance" to more skilled jobs or do work which involved much responsibility. Parker quotes a state employment official who discussed the Farmington Navajo work habits (1954: 20):

After working steadily for two or three weeks, the Navajo has been able to gather enough money for a trip back on the reservation to see his family or attend some kind of ceremonial. Some of them have sheep back there and have to return once in a while to see how they are getting on. He never tells the boss he is going to be gone — I think he is ashamed to or feels that the boss would object and would get angry — so they avoid the entire issue by not saying anything — they just take off.

The wealthiest Navajo in Farmington owned a truck line which hauled vanadium and uranium ore to a mill near Shiprock. Until recently, this individual hired mostly Navajos as truck drivers. At the time of this study, however, he had no Navajo employees because he came to regard them as unreliable. Frequent and unexplained absences from work and unpredictable outbursts of "temperment" contributed to this image. As a result of his attitude, he was thoroughly disliked by other Farmington Navajos.

Parker (1954: 20) gives a statement of an unemployed Farmington Navajo who had been living there for five years. He had been employed steadily until a few months prior to the interview:

They used to have lots of jobs in town — they were pretty easy to get — now this year it's tough to get jobs. It's hard to get jobs since a lot of people moved in from Texas. So we Indians lose the jobs. And there is another thing — some Indian boys work a few days and then quit. Some of them get drunk and do all kinds of things like that. The first thing you know all of the bosses they say that the Indians are no good for work and it's hard for us that got families here to get a job. They think that if some of them do like that — we all do. Lots of Indians have big credit bills with the traders and now they are far behind and can't pay their bills. Right after they lose their jobs he cuts off their credit — he won't carry them if they don't have a job. You see, the trouble is that the young boys don't support families — they just come here to make a little money for themselves and they don't care if they get fired or get drunk.

The "traders" referred to here are those who run trading posts which closely resemble in operation their counterparts in remote areas of the reservation. There are three such stores in Farmington which are patronized by at least 75 per cent of the city's Navajos for a number of reasons. First, the owners and clerks speak Navajo. It is usually easier to get credit here than at the more conventional retail stores in Farmington. One of the traders is an agent who works for the Union Pacific Railroad, and his store is used as an employment agency. Finally, the trading post functions as a communication center. Here the Navajos can often get news about their relatives on the reservation, and they frequently send messages back to kinsmen and friends. These advantages are viewed as outweighing the fact that all trading posts have higher prices than do other Farmington stores. However, some of the younger and more educated Navajos do not patronize the trading posts and show a marked resentment toward them.

The three traders agreed that most Navajos do not spend their money wisely. Too much of their earnings are spent on luxuries such as candy, liquor, and expensive clothing. A husband and wife often have separate credit accounts, especially when they have separate livestock and other resources on the reservation. There are some cases where pooling of purchases would be more economical, but this is not done. There are some instances of two families living together or a single man or woman living with relatives. In both situations, shopping and cooking are done separately. Two of the three traders stated that the majority of town Navajos feel that their main interests and responsibilities are still back on the reservation.

Urban husbands and wives have a number of conflicts which are associated with the wife's diminished economic importance in town and the economic demands made by reservation kinsmen and friends. In town, the husband always makes more money than the wife which usually means that he demands a predominant role in decision-making. This situation is in direct contrast to the reservation where there usually is an equality between spouses or the wife exercises a greater influence in many family affairs. Reservation Navajos frequently visit their Farmington relatives for long periods of time without contributing to the support of the home. The city Navajos resent such prolonged and expensive visits. Where affinal kinsmen are involved, the spouse feels considerably more resentment.

Reservation relatives can also exert economic pressures on their kin in town without coming to visit them. Frequently the former expect the latter to contribute money and food for their welfare. When this is not done, emotional support is withdrawn and the urban family can be made to feel more isolated in their alien environment, since they know that they will not be welcomed at their former reservation homes. Failure to help reservation relatives might well endanger any livestock or other goods which the urban Navajos may have left with their kin.

Children in town tend to restrict the activities of Navajo women much more than they do on the reservation. In contrast to the reservation, children can contribute little or nothing to the support of the family. Both these conditions supplement other uncomfortable pressures felt by their parents.

Parker gives the impression that most of the Farmington Navajos have few relatives in town. Their absence often makes domestic quarrels difficult to reconcile. Male sexual promiscuity and excessive drinking seem to be greater in town than on the reservation.

Parker makes the following comments on Farmington Navajo religious practices (1954: 28):

... the vast majority of town Navajos participate in traditional ceremonials back on the reservation. In the town itself there are no singers. However, there are three hand-tremblers and star gazers who do preliminary diagnosis of the trouble and recommend the type of sing (and sometimes the singer) that should be held. The fees for these services are varied and range from $2.50 to $5.00 in cash and/or various items of food, jewelry, etc. Although almost all of the Navajos in town make use of the regular community medical facilities available there, they also have sings back on the reservation and ... are asked to contribute financially to these ceremonials. ...

Besides sings, the town residents look forward to participating in squaw dances and other religious rites. These provide the occasions to get together with the entire family and participate once more in the Navajo way of life. It is hard to separate this latent function from the more manifest religious functions.

No instances of witchcraft were found in town. Navajo residents appear to believe that witches exist and function on the reservation, but do not affect those living in an urban setting.

Generally Farmington Navajos see no contradiction between an acceptance of Christianity and an adherence to traditional beliefs and practices. Navajos who maintain close relationships with a large extended family are very poor Christians and seldom take part in formal church activities. Navajos who live in town alone or who have broken relations with family members are much more likely to be attracted to Christianity.

The most frequent causes of arrest among local Navajos are fighting and driving while drunk. Drinking seems to be most serious for those in the eighteen to twenty-four-year-age group. Few or no crimes are committed by sober Navajos. Although by 1954 it was legal for Navajos to buy liquor in a public bar, most Navajos still preferred to buy a bottle and drink with other Navajos in a relatively secluded place. A Navajo does not like to drink alone. When drunk, Farmington Navajos never fight with Anglos. Other Navajos, and occasionally the few local Negroes, are usually involved. Sexual infidelity is a common cause of fighting.

A few Navajo girls were working as full-time prostitutes. At the time of Parker's study, there was a growing incidence of venereal disease. Many resident Navajos, especially the women, suffer from hypochondria.

Movies, drinking, and, for the men, gambling are common recreational outlets. Both sexes enjoy watching the local school teams participate in various kinds of sports events.

Parker comments briefly on Navajo-Navajo relationships in Farmington (1954: 35):

Social relationships on the reservation were governed almost completely by traditionally accepted role obligations with the nuclear family, the extended family, and the clan. In addition social sanctions were applied mainly by relatives who lived close by. In towns, families come to live without extended family relatives and clan relationship becomes almost meaningless in the new environment. As a result there are few established patterns of cooperation that have been worked out in

town, nor is there any degree of identification with one another as Navajos who share common problems. This coupled with the fact that no new leadership patterns have emerged in the Farmington Navajo community makes it almost impossible for the Indians as a group to engage in any collective self-assertive action. There is little cohesiveness or identification with common symbols among the town Navajo.

He (p. 36) also discusses Navajo-Anglo relationships:

. . . the Navajo population in Farmington are (and feel) isolated from most of the non-Indian population. Increasingly, they are becoming sensitive to the fact that they are being discriminated against because they are Indians. The specific complaints (by Navajos) that I have heard are that the police force treats them much harsher than it does the non-Indian population, employers prefer to give jobs to white laborers, and bartenders and shopkeepers are sometimes rude to them. Thus, in effect, the town Navajos are excluded from active participation in their reservation communities and town community.

About four years ago, a Farmington Navajo Club was organized, but nothing is known about its activities.

CORTEZ, COLORADO

McPhee's report states that there were 54 Navajos in Cortez in 1951, a total which includes adults and children. There were eight family units, one single man, and eight single women. The families had lived here continuously for an average of three and one-half years. Most Navajos had a history of frequent migration in search of work, but they usually returned to Cortez. At least a dozen Navajo families came to Cortez in the summer and fall months to work in the harvests.

Housing was of poor quality. Three families lived in tents, one in a hogan, and another in a cellar. Four families lived in frame houses.

Navajos took little or no part in community functions. Most of the children attended local public schools. A few Navajos were arrested occasionally for drunkenness.

RICO, COLORADO

Rico is a lead and zinc mining town. According to Luebben (1955: 46), as of November, 1953, Rico had a total population of 335. One hundred seventeen of this number were Navajos, and 75 of this aggregate were miners. There were 72 Anglo miners.

The rest of the population were women and children.

A few Navajos had come to work in Rico when the mine opened in 1928. Up to 1942, a total of less than 50 had worked in the mine. The number of Navajos employed was positively correlated with the demand for zinc and lead ore.

Navajos have never regarded Rico as a home, but merely a place to work for a short time to earn money when conditions are especially difficult on the reservation. Very few work here for more than one year at a time. When they leave town they usually return to the reservation. Navajo miners have difficulty handling their pay and rarely save anything. Their checks are usually sent directly to the general store to be balanced off against their current debts. Navajos are competent miners and are able to learn the various skills associated with mining operations. However, all Navajos show an unwillingness to accept responsibility. There is a high rate of turnover in personnel and considerable absenteeism due to heavy drinking and frequent visits to the reservation.

Navajos and Anglos associate only while working in the mine. Few Navajos speak or understand English. They resent Anglos because they feel that Navajos have been given poorer housing and get lower pay for doing the same sort of work as Anglos. This, however, is not the case. Anglos also refuse to do favors for them. Anglo miners do not like Navajos because of their poor command of English, general bad health, and careless sanitary habits.

Elsewhere, Luebben (1964: 9–10) states:

Discrimination against Navajos was present in company, mercantile, and other situations. Personal discrimination is apparent in all sorts of contexts involving a choice. Aside from necessary economic interaction, two mutually exclusive, parallel aggregates [Navajo and Anglo] existed within but do not share the facilities of [Rico].

Navajos come to Rico to work because they want money to buy such Anglo goods as pick-up trucks and fancy clothing and satisfy their obligations on the reservation such as supporting ceremonial functions and providing hospitality for friends and relatives. Luebben (1955: 8) states that many Navajos favor mining in Rico rather than mining on the reservation because the former pays higher wages. The mining company recruits Navajos on an informal basis. Navajos returning to the reservation often urge their associates to come to Rico because it is near the reservation, and mining per se, despite the element of danger, is relatively pleasant labor. Most Rico Navajos come from the "San Juan strip," as the Toadlena-Tocito area and the Lukachukai-Red Rock area are called (Luebben 1955: 48).

Most Navajo miners are under thirty-five and have extremely limited educational and job experience. The majority bring their families with them. At the time of Luebben's study in 1953–54, no single Navajos lived in Rico. Most of the Rico Navajos are related on the basis of consanguineal or affinal ties. Navajo children complain about the lack of recreation facilities in town, but feel that the reservation is worse in this respect. There is a public school, but it offers only eight years of education.

Luebben (1955: 342) found no evidence of witchcraft. He notes that Navajos are often "mean and aggressive" when drunk. One Navajo was shot and killed when he attacked an Anglo storekeeper.

SUMMARY AND CONCLUSIONS

BIA sources have estimated that within the last 50 to 60 years more than 150,000 Indians voluntarily left their reservations. During the past twelve fiscal years (1952 through 1963), nearly 30,000 Indian workers have moved to various cities under the relocation program. About 17,000 or 60 per cent of these people have become permanently employed, presumably in cities. With the data at hand it is impossible to determine if the federal relocation program has stimulated off-reservation movement or simply has made migration more convenient for those who would have moved anyway. At any rate the relocation program is far from solving the two critical problems facing American Indians today: chronic unemployment and the impossibility for an exploding population to subsist on constantly diminishing reservation resources.

Dozier, Simpson, and Yinger (1957: 165) have reached a number of broad conclusions regarding integration and assimilation of American Indians in the larger society, conclusions which this chapter has tentatively confirmed:

(1) Indian groups residing on reservations (homelands) will continue indefinitely as distinct social units; (2) although Indian communities resist assimilation, they are constantly making adjustments to life around them; (3) although Indian cultures, as self-contained systems, will probably disappear eventually, this fact does not seem to many Indians to be "a reason for abandoning their present way of life"; (4) optional assimilation on

an individual basis, unlike forced assimilation, would leave the way open for assimilation to occur "at the speed and in the direction which the people themselves desire"; (5) even though many Indians continue to live in separate communities with some distinctive cultural patterns, integration into the life of the larger society can still take place.

It can be said that the data in this chapter generally confirm the hypotheses posed in Chapter 1 of this study. There are permanent-resident, Anglo-modified, and traditional Indians from all of the tribes and in all of the cities which have been considered. The specific nature of these three categories, which can also be viewed as orientations on an individual level, may vary from tribe to tribe and possibly from city to city, but the available data lack the depth necessary to indicate this variation in detail. The sparsity of data also makes it impossible to determine why a given individual assumes a particular orientation; Indians who are permanent residents may have become so for similar or identical reasons, but this is far from certain. It seems evident that reservation or urban residence per se means little as far as assimilation is concerned.

With the exception of the Yaqui of Tucson, who are to be regarded as political refugees, Indians generally come to the cities for economic reasons. Reservation resources, at best, have been inadequate and the steady increase of the Indian population since 1900 has intensified this condition. Hence Indians who are capable of earning a living in an urban situation leave the reservations and work in cities for varying lengths of time. Most Indians who are capable of earning a living in a city are young adults, have reasonably good health, and either have acquired a marketable skill or are able to acquire one in a short time. The majority of urban Indians would prefer to live on their particular reservations because, while city living can provide the material necessities of life, it denies them the emotional support of Indian friends and relatives, a more relaxed and permissive cycle of work and recreation, the opportunity to carry out various traditional behavioral roles as Indians, and other things which they highly value. This denial, when compounded by unpleasant experiences in the city and/or compelling attractions on the reservation, may cause an Indian to return to his home despite the conscious awareness that such a move constitutes economic suicide.

Of course, it seems reasonable to conclude that some Indians leave the reservation for the city for other reasons than that of securing a satisfactory job and that Indians in this group who return to the reservation do so because city living becomes oppressive for one reason or another. This chapter has suggested that many single, young Indians may come to the city *via* the relocation program simply for the sake of adventure and have no intention of eventually acquiring a greater degree of economic independence.

The data here pose important questions which cannot be answered by this study. Do off-reservation seasonal workers differ qualitatively from more or less permanent urban migrants? Adams' Shonto Navajos do appear to differ from the long-term Indian residents of the larger cities (1963). Are there any significant differences between Indian reservation border town residents and those living in cities some distance from a reservation? Several instances have been cited where urban residence appears to have heightened a sense of Indian identity. Does this increased awareness result in an eventual return to the reservation? Does it contribute to a better or worse urban adjustment? Are there any significant tribal differentials with regard to urban residence and adjustment? The comparative material in this chapter suggest that there may well be, but nothing definite can be said in this regard.

To understand fully the significance of Indian urban residence for a given Indian or group of Indians a number of factors must be considered. Tribal identity, idiosyncratic characteristics, the reservation, the urban situation, and the conditions of migration are among them.

Using the above comparative material as a backdrop, this study explores these factors as they function in one specific case — a small number of Navajos living in Albuquerque, New Mexico.

Obviously, more generalizations can be made regarding urban Indians than have been given here. However, it is felt that a more meaningful discussion can be effected after the Albuquerque data have been presented.

3.   THE BACKGROUND

THIS CHAPTER will provide a background for viewing the Albuquerque Navajo data. This material consists of a number of factors: (1) the Southwest and the people of the Southwest; (2) other Indian enclaves; (3) the Navajo enclave; and (4) the city of Albuquerque and its occupants. A comprehensive description of these factors is well beyond the scope of this study, and factors (2) and (3) have been slighted. It is intended here only to indicate the nature and the extent of the complexity of the data. The general sociocultural and temporal dimensions of the background are emphasized to provide a necessary perspective for the study of the Albuquerque Navajos.

THE SOUTHWEST

Most anthropologists, like Spicer (1962), agree that the Southwest consists of the northern half of the Mexican states of Chihuahua and Sonora, plus Arizona and New Mexico. There is general consensus that this area has a distinctive unity, but the nature of this unity and its precise spacial distribution remains a matter of considerable debate (Haury 1954). Spicer (1962: 1–4) considers the Southwest to be an enclave of native peoples whose present nature is the product of 427 years (1533–1960) of Spanish, Mexican, and North American contact. Climate and other natural influences make the area a regional entity.

The Southwest in 1960 had an Indian population of about 200,000. Twenty-five Indian groups having some degree of distinctive custom lived here. Each of these groups lived under a wide variety of conditions with respect to the natural and cultural environment. The processes through which the Indian enclaves had become realities were indeed complex.

The remainder of this section is devoted to only a part of the Southwest — the states of Arizona and New Mexico. Current Navajo activity and influence in the rest of the Southwest area is virtually non-existent.

According to the 1960 Census, the total population of Arizona was 1,302,161. There were 83,387 Indians, 43,403 Negroes, and 1,169,517 Anglos. The figure for Indians is probably too low, since the enumeration of this category involves difficulties which are not found with Anglos and Negroes. Spanish-speaking people were merged with Anglos. Most of the Anglos and Negroes were found in or near the cities of Tucson and Phoenix. Phoenix had 8,136 Indians and Tucson, 7,307. The rest of the state's Indians were probably living on or near the various reservations. The Indian tribes of Arizona are Navajo, Hopi, Paiute, Havasupai, Walapai, Mohave, Chemehuevi, Yavapai, Apache, Yuma, Cocopa, Papago, Pima, and Maricopa. The largest tribes in terms of population as of 1962 were Navajo, 52,000; Apache, 8,365; Pima and Maricopa, 6,125; Hopi, 5,176; Papago, 5,040. It should be noted that the totals for each tribe represent those who are recorded in the tribal rolls. Registration here is independent of residence.

The 1960 Census states that the population of New Mexico was 951,023. There were 56,255 Indians, 17,063 Negroes, and 875,763 Anglos. As was the case with Arizona, Spanish-speaking people were merged with Anglos. Most of the Anglos and Negroes lived in Albuquerque, Santa Fe, and smaller urban centers. In the state's urban areas about 10,303 Indians were found, while about 45,000 lived in rural places. The majority of New Mexico's urban Indians lived in the following cities: Gallup, 2,061; Albuquerque, 1,848; Farmington, 484; Santa Fe, 344; and Grants, 120. The remainder were found in Alamogordo, Artesia, Carlsbad, Clovis, Hobbs, Las Cruces, Los Alamos, Roswell, and towns of smaller size. For a number of reasons, all figures having to do with Indians are probably too conservative.

The Indian "tribes" of New Mexico are the Rio Grande Pueblos (Tesuque, Taos, Santo Domingo, Santa Clara, Santa Ana, San Juan, San

Ildefonso, San Felipe, Sandia, Pojoaque, Picuris, Nambe, Jemez, Isleta, Zia, and Cochiti), Western Pueblos (Acoma with three sub-villages and Laguna with five sub-villages and Zuni), Navajo, and Apache. The populations of these groups are as follows: the Rio Grande Pueblos, 13,202; the Western Pueblos, 8,880; Navajo, 20,000; Apache, 2,711.

INDIAN — NON-INDIAN RELATIONS

Spicer (1962: 371–563) comments at length on the political incorporation, linguistic unification, community reorientation, religious diversification, and economic integration of the various Indian enclaves to the enveloping societies. Since linguistic unification and religious diversification are of little relevance to this study, they are not discussed.

The process of political incorporation involved two kinds of adjustment. A kind of political assimilation occurred which amounted to a progressive adoption by Indians of forms of political organization similar to those of the invading and dominant peoples. A form of political adaptation also occurred whereby new forms of organization arose which functioned as channels of communication and cooperation between Indian communities and the surrounding non-Indian societies (Spicer 1962: 419).

Spicer's remarks regarding Anglo-Indian incorporation are of special relevance since they indicate how the current Indian reservation situation evolved as a response to Anglo influences. Indians were placed on reservations. These areas were remote enough to discourage occupation by Anglos. The creation of reservations controlled by federal influences led to strong feelings of tribal identity, a general breakdown of local group organization, and the growth of deep feelings of dependence on the BIA. Because of the nature of aboriginal settlement patterns and certain historical factors, a few groups such as the Navajos, Papagos, and Eastern Pueblos escaped this general process of social disintegration, but the problem was deep-rooted in the other groups. The BIA instituted tribal councils, hoping to encourage political organization and thus counter the effects of this advanced community disintegration. The goal was only partially realized. From the earliest time of Anglo domination an unstable political adaptation rather than a progressive assimilation was characteristic of Indian communities in New Mexico and Arizona, producing conditions satisfactory to neither Indians nor Anglos.

Indian community reorientation followed no general pattern. During the 350-year contact period the varieties of integration into wider social units for all Indian communities ranged from a close cohesion with the general society to a tenuous linkage with the broader social horizon. But whatever the kind of prevailing relationship to the non-Indian world, by the twentieth century Indian settlements were no longer autonomous and self-sufficient.

Much of this dependency was of an economic nature. The general economic base had shifted from intensive agriculture supplemented by hunting and gathering to wage work augmented by livestock production among some groups and by small-scale cash-crop farming among others. A prominent feature of this change was a general reliance on material goods produced outside the Indian communities.

This economic integration with the greater Anglo society will probably have little direct effect on the continuing maintenance of Indian settlements and the distinctive ethnic identity of the residents of these communities. The survival of native groups, despite successful conquests by invaders and vigorous programs by the conquerors for cultural assimilation of the native group, in the light of human history seems to be a common phenomenon.

NAVAJO — NON-NAVAJO RELATIONS

The relationships currently existing between reservation Navajos and non-Navajos are exceedingly complex. For the purposes of this study, a superficial examination of the situation is adequate. Kluckhohn and Leighton (1951: 75–8) provide a good general discussion of this topic, which foreshadows some of the material to follow.

Until World War II the majority of Navajos had little contact with Anglos. In many of the more remote parts of the reservation today such contact remains limited to a few traders and government employees. Despite this relative isolation, about 20,000 Navajos left their reservation during the War to serve in the armed forces or to work for wages for extended periods of time. Such activities have stimulated the spread of Anglo ideas to a considerable extent.

The relation of Navajos with other Indians is largely conditioned by geography. The Pueblos, Paiutes, Utes, Yumans, and Apaches trade with the Navajos. Trade goods consist largely of food stuffs, manufactured items such as baskets and jewelry, and ceremonial equipment. All of the above groups show a good deal of mutual interest in each other's ceremonies in the form of attendance and occasionally even participation. Purely social contacts also occur and, along with ceremonial and economic contacts, promote the general exchange of ideas and information. Contacts have also occurred in recent years in off-reservation boarding schools. These varieties of inter-action have resulted in some sense of solidarity with all other Indians in spite of animosities and cultural differences of considerable dimension and duration.

Navajos categorize non-Indians as "Mexicans" (Spanish Americans), "Anglos," Texans, and Mormons. At times sympathetic bonds are felt with Mexicans by virtue of the fact that both are members of subordinate groups. Mexicans will not only sell Navajos liquor, but occasionally will give it to them and even shelter them from the Anglo police. A Mexican who believes that he has been attacked by a witch will sometimes go to a Navajo singer to be treated. Hostile inter-group relations exist with equal frequency, usually taking the form of pervasive distrust and open brawls. Texans and Mormons are regarded with a kind of humorous distaste. Anglos or non-Spanish-speaking Caucasians are divided into the two sub-categories of good and bad people. The former consists of traders, missionaries, and anthrolopogists, while the latter is composed of Indian Service employees, off-reservation police, and border town merchants.

The Navajo attitude toward Negroes varies from one of mild contempt to a pervasive hatred. Griffith (1960) proposes the idea that this feeling ultimately stems from a Navajo identification with Anglos. Those of my Navajo informants who were questioned about this situation gave two explanations: First, many Navajos have had unfortunate experiences with Negro bootleggers in the various reservation border towns, and, second, a large proportion of the BIA school teachers on the reservation are Negro. For many Navajos, their first painful contacts with the indoctrination of "standard Anglo" codes of behavior occur through these teachers. The resentment engendered by this experience can carry over into the adult years. Obviously, the origins and development of this attitude are complex and certainly worthy of systematic study.

THE NAVAJO ENCLAVE

Navajo country consists of three small communities,

the Checkerboard area, and the large reservation. These places will be described in terms of their geographic relationship to Albuquerque.

Alamo is a small community of 350 Navajos which is located about eighty-five miles due southwest of Albuquerque. These Navajos live on allotted lands and have been isolated from the main body of Navajos for about 100 years, according to Van Valkenburgh (1941: 117). The total area of holdings would probably not exceed forty square miles of barren, unproductive agricultural land interspersed with high mesas and lava flows. Spanish-speaking ranchers surround the community and are the source of many conflicts. Subsistence is marginal and life is sustained by a combination of farming, seasonal labor, and relief.

Canyoncito, a small reservation of ninety square miles of terrain similar in nature to that of Alamo, lies 30 miles west of Albuquerque. According to Kurtz (1963: 258) about 600 people "live" here, but no more than 215 people are in residence for the majority of the year, largely because of the demands of off-reservation seasonal labor. As in the case of Alamo, subsistence is marginal. Available natural resources and traditional subsistence practices cannot support the population. Accordingly, survival also depends upon a combination of agriculture, off-reservation work, and relief.

Ramah is a community of about 400 Navajos who live on allotted lands fifty miles south of Gallup and twenty-four miles east of Zuni Pueblo. Total land holdings do not exceed that of Alamo and Canyoncito. Anglo encroachment on lands is a constant threat.

Approximately 150 miles to the west of Albuquerque lies the Checkerboard area. This 7,000-square-mile area in New Mexico (see Fig. 2) is about 50 miles wide and inhabited by at least 20,000 Navajos occupying allotted lands, interspersed with Anglo ranches and large areas of public domain. Living conditions here are no better than in the three areas discussed above. Constant friction occurs with Anglo and Spanish-speaking settlers over water and grazing lands.

The main Navajo reservation, whose eastern boundary lies about 200 miles to the west of Albuquerque, occupies an area of 24,000 square miles in northeastern Arizona, southern Utah, and western New Mexico. About 50,000 Navajos live here. This area, like the others, is overcrowded and underdeveloped. Subsistence conditions are as austere as in the other Navajo areas. One of the important differences between the main reservation and the other areas discussed is greater isolation from non-Navajo influences and conflicts. However, with the gradual development of all-weather roads and anticipated industrialization, this relative isolation may soon disappear.

In summary, an aggregate of 80,000 Navajos (1965 population estimates are slightly over 100,-000) maintain a marginal existence in a precarious and hostile physical and social environment. Life for these people has been such for at least the past thirty years and may well continue to be so for several generations more.

4. THE URBAN-RESERVATION SYSTEM

As was stated earlier, it seems evident that for a given Navajo the reservation and the city form parts of the same whole or system. Non-permanent Navajos occupy a sometimes stable, and sometimes shifting place in it. For purposes of the study, this urban and reservation Navajo system can be said to consist of two inter-related orbits, a reservation orbit and an urban orbit. Non-permanent Navajos simultaneously experience push and pull forces in relation to both the reservation orbit and the urban orbit. Hence, a description of both environments is necessary for an understanding of what is to follow.

THE RESERVATION ORBIT

Here emphasis is given to the factors of location, occupants and their activities, impinging forces, and probable future development. Today, the reservation generally consists of two types of communities which impinge upon supporting areas of variable size: the traditional community and the "transitional" community. The latter term is used by Shepardson and Hammond (1964: 1029):

Transitional communities such as Shiprock, Navajo, Fort Defiance, and Tuba City are variously supported by oil extraction, mining, lumbering, other wage-work interests, and irrigated farming.

This same source characterizes traditional communities as being "geographically isolated communities where herding and marginal agriculture offer the only way of making a living and traditional ways are the mode." In Firth's terminology (1954: 49) both types are *sectional* small communities. Until about forty years ago before the advent of pervasive Anglo influence there were many *integral* small communities in Navajo country, found for the most part in the western half of the reservation. It is conceivable but unlikely that permanent-resident Navajos could be produced by traditional communities. Anglo-modified Navajos may come from either traditional or transitional communities, but the latter would

seem more likely. The reverse is the case for traditional Navajos.

Shepardson and Hammond (1964: 1031–49) provide a concise but comprehensive description of Rainbow Plateau, the archetype of a traditional community. Their periods of fieldwork (the summers of 1960, 1961, and 1962) overlap with mine in Albuquerque. The community has a population of 323 Navajos who occupy an area of approximately 150 square miles. The nature of the land is such that it is suitable only for grazing and marginal dry farming. Potable water is extremely limited and there are no known mineral deposits of commercial value. The resident Anglo population as of 1961 was eight: two trading couples, a trading post employee, a missionary couple, and a woman school teacher. There are no influences for immediate drastic change on the part of the BIA, the Tribal Council, or the Navajo residents. Rainbow Plateau is still isolated and will probably remain so for an indefinite period of time.

Social life in this community closely follows a traditional pattern. Shepardson and Hammond state that

[social life] . . . was focused upon pastoralism and marginal agriculture. Scattered residence patterns, with seasonal moves for pasture and water, for planting and harvesting, within a defined area, was the rule. The extended family consisting of parents, unmarried children, and married children, typically married daughters with their families, was the basic unit for subsistence and residence. Navajo social structure was flexible and permitted patrilocal and neolocal, as well as matrilocal residence. A wide network of clan relationships (an individual being a member of his mother's clan but "born for" his father's clan) with exogamic rules which forbade marriage into his own clan, into his father's clan, or with a person who was born for the same clan as one was born for, served to tie each Navajo and each family into the loose sociocultural system of the tribe. Non-coercive authority for directing economic activities was exercised by the head of an extended family. A Headman acted as arbiter in disputes and as spokesman for a little community. Specific authority for specific occasions was exercised by the Singer during a curing ceremony, a leader of the hunt, and, before the Conquest, by the war leader. . . .

The value system emphasized the desirability of harmonious relations within the extended family, hard work, the acquisition of property, generosity, self-control, and reasonableness. The philosophy was pragmatic, directed to the here-and-now, and was characterized . . . as "familistic individualism". . . .

The present community income . . . derives from the traditional economy and supplementary income from wage work, welfare, and free services. The basic economic orientation of Rainbow Plateau is to pastoralism and marginal agriculture. (1034)

Every family has use rights to small patches of land for dry farms on the plateau, or for small scale irrigated plots in the canyons. Agricultural techniques are simple, requiring only a few hand tools. Corn, melons, and peaches are the principal crops; these products are not sold commercially but may be bartered with neighbors and relatives. . . .

Most women weave rugs and a few make wedding baskets and wicker bottles covered with pitch, which they sell to the trading posts. Men make moccasins, leather halters, and lariats for family use or barter only. A few individuals occasionally rent horses to tourists.

Shepardson and Hammond (1035) say that two individuals were working outside the community.

There are four permanent wage work jobs, and one part time job, held by Rainbow Plateauans at the Navajo Mountain School, where they are employed as cooks, janitor, and dormitory attendants. . . . Other wage work is on specific projects [e.g., the salary for holding a Chapter office, being chairman of the grazing committee, etc.]. . . . Most of the employment is provided on emergency work projects financed by the Navajo Tribal Council and planned by the local Chapter. . . . The total work per man for a year ranges from one to six weeks. This is a highly desired form of employment which can easily be absorbed by a sheep herding family. . . .

[The] extended family serves as the basic cooperating group for herding and farming and residence. The residence group, or camp, consists of clusters of hogans "within shouting distance of each other," each of these hogans typically sheltering a biological family. For larger enterprises, such as the big ceremonies, clan relatives on both maternal and paternal sides, affinals, and neighbors will be asked to assist. . . .

The number of hogans in a camp varied from 1 to 8. . . .

The most frequently found type of camp in 1961 follows the traditional pattern of component nuclear families living with the wife's parents or her matrilineal kinsmen, there being 9 such *matrilocal* camps on Rainbow Plateau. There are 5 camps made up of a single nuclear family in *neolocal* residence. One camp is *patri-*

local, being composed of a couple and their married son, his wife and children. There are 6 mixed camps, in which some component couples are living matrilocally, while others are living patrilocally. . . .

Shepardson and Hammond complete the description with remarks on Navajo society, socialization, and a general assessment of the viability of the community:

Navajo culture is a compound of conservatism and plasticity. The indigenous system has never institutionalized the desirability of change per se. Children are discouraged from showing initiative or assuming authority. Mental stimulation is not valued. At the same time, the extreme flexibility of Navajo social structure, which offers preferred patterns of grouping, residence and role behavior, while tolerating a number of alternates is institutionalized and expressed as the value, "It's up to him." Navajo society is accomplishment-oriented. Its members are more interested in getting a particular job done than they are in preserving the vested interests of types of groups or roles. They do not wish to be White men, therefore they do not see themselves as deprived. The older Navajos on Rainbow Plateau compare their lot with the lean days of their childhood, or with their grandparents' tales of hardships during and after the Conquest. Many of the young people see Rainbow Plateau as a privileged region, which runs the danger of attracting malevolent, jealous witchcraft "because we have so many nice fat sheep". . . .

Socialization of the children, during the first six years of life before they leave for boarding school, and afterwards during summer vacations, effectively inculcates the traditional beliefs and loyalties which insure adequate motivation for filling the requisite societal roles. Young men, despite modern education, still learn to herd sheep, ride horses, drive wagons, and plant farms. Young women learn to herd, to weave, to make mutton stew, "fry bread," "kneel-down bread," and to bake in earth ovens huge sun-rise cakes for the puberty ceremony. . . .

Rainbow Plateau retains all of the action systems which met the functional requisites of the traditional society. The alien authority systems in which it participates provide alternates and supplements, which served to support, rather than replace, the traditional structure. Persistence, therefore, is more deep-going than is change in this little community. . . .

Adams (1963: 30–148) offers a description of Shonto, a community which appears to be quite similar to Rainbow Plateau, except that most of the men did seasonal, off-reservation wage work. Adams' field work was carried out during the period 1954–56. There are several other communities which are perhaps not as conservative as Rainbow Plateau and Shonto, but they certainly can be classed as traditional. These are Copper Mine, Kaibito, Piute,

Oljeto, Goldtooth, Gospel Mission, Dinnebito, Tolani Lake, Castle Butte, Dilkon, Cedar Spring, White Cone, Tselani, Black Mountain, Rough Rock, Chilchinbito, Rock Point, Round Rock, Nazlini, Oak Springs, Crystal, Iyanbito, Smith Lake, Pueblo Bonito, Huerfano, Red Rock, and Cove. There may well be others, but these make up the majority. They have at least three characteristics in common: First, each is located away from all-weather roads; second, potential for industrial or commercial development of each is low or non-existent; third, they are distributed uniformly over the reservation. (Fig. 2).

Shepardson (1961: 1–3) provides a useful description of Shiprock in 1960, a transitional community which was "active, articulate, politically sophisticated, and bellicose."

Shiprock, New Mexico, is the most acculturated community on the Navajo Reservation. It is an unincorporated settlement at the juncture of two paved highways near the Four Corners where Arizona, Utah, Colorado and New Mexico meet. Shiprock proper has about 1,500 Navajo and 300 white residents. Shiprock Precinct, which elects a councilman to the Navajo Tribal Council, has an estimated population of 3,000 and the Shiprock Subagency of the Indian Bureau comprises about 10,000. Shiprock proper has permanent water suitable for irrigation from the San Juan River. The San Juan Basin is rich in oil, natural gas, helium, vanadium, uranium and coal. The bulk of the Navajo Tribal income is derived from oil and gas leases and royalties from this area. In Shiprock proper, Federal and Tribal offices, an irrigation headquarters, a farm training center, a hospital, a courthouse and jail, a Chapter House, and four schools comprise government facilities. A branch bank, stores, restaurants, hotels, a Tribal-owned motel and restaurant, and a movie furnish commercial services. Local industry consists of seven small coal mines, a sand and gravel pit, Kerr-McGee's uranium processing plant, a helium plant operated by the Bureau of Mines, and ... the Arizona Light and Power Company's electric plant. Six Christian missions serve the settlement. Reservation-wise, Shiprock is a metropolis. . . .

Navajos here earn their living as sheep herders, in part as irrigation farmers, as small businessmen (one store, three service stations and a garage), operators of the coal mines, and as wage workers. There are possibly 350 permanent jobs. The most secure positions are with the Indian Bureau and the U. S. Public Health Service. The Navajo Tribe provides good, but less secure, positions. Sixty-five Navajos work for Kerr-McGee, and two, as janitors, work for the Bureau of Mines. Construction of schools and buildings offers temporary employment, as attraction to outsiders. Railroads and ranches provide seasonal labor openings, but automation has drastically reduced opportunities for Navajo employment.

Welfare payments and Tribal public works help to support others. Ambitious plans for development of resources have been made by Bureau and Tribe. For example, it is expected that 10,000 acres will be irrigated from Navajo Dam. . . .

Shiprock has long been a center of conflicts of varying sorts arising from acculturative pressures. . . . Present-day political conflicts operate at three levels: in the general elections for state and federal offices, in the Navajo Tribal Council and in the Shiprock Chapter.

In addition to the transitional communities named above there are Chinle, Crownpoint, Ganado, Kayenta, Teec Nos Pos, Aneth, Fruitland, and Fort Defiance. For the most part these places are in the eastern half of the reservation. Their industrial development is problematical. They are on or near all-weather roads. (Fig. 2)

These transitional communities are the places where urban resident Anglo-modified Navajos hope to live, and where many such Navajos now live. They offer Anglo-modified Navajos a range of material comforts, education, and medical facilities generally inferior to those available in the city. However, they lack many of the city's disadvantages, and hence they are perceived as desirable.

The capacity of these communities to absorb additional Navajos is limited or non-existent. An increased capacity would seem to depend upon increased industrialization. This, in turn, hinges around the interest of private capital and the skill of tribal and federal officials in attracting industry. The current industrial development of the reservation is at best minimal.

A significant change of status will probably not occur soon. Only in the last five years have limited natural gas, power, and oil lines been laid across the periphery of the reservation. In addition to the plants listed above, Kaiser Aluminum and a plastics firm have very small units southeast of Window Rock. The BVD corporation may build a plant soon in the Shiprock area which will employ 800 Navajos and have an annual payroll of $2,000,000. The sawmill at Navajo might possibly meet tribal expectations as a source of revenue and employment.

There are, however, definite obstacles which discourage private capital from coming to the reservation. Transportation and water resources are wholly inadequate. Prospects for their adequate development are poor. The available labor force — the 13,000 "unemployed and underemployed" resident adults — is unskilled, and many workers unemployable for various reasons. It is difficult to induce non-Navajo skilled workers to remain on the reservation for any length of time because of such unfavorable living conditions as a high cost of living, the absence of conventional recreational facilities, and marginal or poor living quarters. The actions of the tribal government are unpredictable and, in the past, have been inimical to outside interests as in 1954 when the Tribe confiscated the physical plants of all traders on the reservation. Since that time a trader has been able to own only merchandise.

It is possible for Anglo-modified Navajos to follow a non-traditional existence on the reservation in an area which is outside of a traditional or transitional community. The *Navajo Times* (July 8, 1962: 7) describes a curio shop owned and operated by three Navajo brothers near Lupton, Arizona, close to Highway 66. They have had several years of off-reservation living experience. Reservation adjustments of this sort are rare, however.

THE URBAN ORBIT

THE CITY OF ALBUQUERQUE

Albuquerque was founded in 1706 as a Spanish villa on the banks of the Rio Grande. It was a way-station of the Chihuahua trail, the life-line between Santa Fe, the provincial Capital, and Mexico City. The present city grew up around the Santa Fe Railway Station, about two miles east of the old villa, and was built in the late 1880's. The new town was laid out when the rails reached this point on their way to the Pacific coast. It soon became a wool marketing center and was incorporated in 1890.

Albuquerque is noted as a health and tourist center, but its principal business has always been the distribution of goods and services. It is the center for the state's conventions, insurance agencies, hospital and medical facilities, government agencies, livestock industry, general contracting, and home of the state university and the state fair.

The city is an important terminal point and headquarters for large shops of the Atchinson, Topeka, and Santa Fe Railway. The Santa Fe employs an average of 1,200 people at an average annual payroll of more than $6,000,000. The Albuquerque airport was the nation's third busiest in 1959. The federal government maintains fifteen district or regional offices here.

Following the establishment of the Los Alamos Laboratory during World War II, the atomic energy program in the state grew rapidly, particularly in the Albuquerque area where program-related installations are numerous. An Atomic Energy Commission field headquarters is located at Sandia Base for administering programs for research, development, testing, production and storage of nuclear weapons and for administering peacetime atomic programs. The center has fourteen area and branch offices ranging from the Pacific to the east coast, and an extensive contractor complex. About 760 employees work in Albuquerque with an annual payroll of approximately $5,800,000.

A Defense Atomic Support Agency is responsible for assisting the field agency of the Atomic Energy Commission and the military services in the development of atomic weapons with the desired military characteristics. This agency participates with the AEC in atomic tests to determine the effects of military weapons on military personnel, equipment, and facilities. The organization known as Sandia Base is a part of Field Command DASA. It is commanded by an army officer and provides all the support services rendered by the normal military post.

The AEC Sandia Laboratory, which is operated at Sandia Base for the AEC by Sandia Corporation, a Western Electric Co. subsidiary, has approximately 8,000 employees earning more than $58,000,000 per year and is the state's largest non-governmental employer. The Laboratory is concerned principally with non-nuclear phases of atomic weapons development. Kirtland Air Force Base is the home of the Air Force Special Weapons Center, the Naval Air Special Weapons Facility, the 34th Air Division (Defense), and the New Mexico Air National Guard's 188th Fighter-Interceptor Squadron. As part of the Air Research and Development Command, Special Weapons Center scientists and engineers carry out nuclear weapons research and development, "mating" bombs to aircraft and warheads to rockets and missiles, and conducting studies of radiation and blast effect. The 34th Air Division, a part of the Air Defense Command, operates radar sites in the area, and the 93rd Fighter-Interceptor Squadron provides the air defense of this section of the Southwest.

Kirtland employs 2,200 civilian workers, with an average monthly payroll in excess of $650,000. There are nearly 5,000 officers and airmen assigned to the base, with a military payroll of $1,300,000 per month. Kirtland, which is jointly used by the military, airlines, and private pilots, has four runways, the largest of which is nearly two-and-a-half miles long.

An AEC production facility, the AEC South Albuquerque Works, is operated under contract by ACF Industries, Inc., and employs more than 2,000 people with a payroll of more than $12,000,000 per year.

The labor force in Albuquerque is comprised mainly of non-migratory native workers, families moving in for climate and opportunity reasons, and many highly-trained people employed by the several AEC projects and the AEC sub-contractors.

The estimated division of the labor force is summarized in Table 2.

TABLE 2
THE ALBUQUERQUE LABOR FORCE

Type of Employment	Number Employed
Contract Construction	7300
Manufacturing	7200
Transportation, Communication, and Utilities	6000
Trade	17400
Finance, Insurance, and Real Estate	4100
Service and Miscellaneous (including Sandia Laboratory)	15900
Government	16400
All other Non-Agricultural Employment (self employed and family workers)	8200
Agricultural	700
TOTAL	90200

Source: Greater Albuquerque Chamber of Commerce, 1960.

Over 350 small manufacturing firms of wide diversity are located in the area served by the Greater Albuquerque Chamber of Commerce. Most recent manufacturing installations involve cement and gypsum products. The total employment of all manufacturing, fabricating, and processing plants in Bernalillo County for the last quarter of 1959 exceeded 7,684 and provided a payroll of $9,278,408.

Albuquerque's potential for expansion is limited by two crucial factors: a shortage of water for commercial purposes and remoteness from urban areas of greater industrial development. Its economic future is problematical. An Albuquerque Economic Supports Analysis (1958: v) seems to characterize the situation realistically when it says that the principal block to Albuquerque's economic development is the fact that too many workers are now on various federal payrolls. A recent report published by the Bureau of Business Research of the University of New Mexico (1962: 3–4) suggests that the economies of the city and state are no longer expand-

ing at the rate of the previous decade because of the decrease in defense spending and a decline in capital spending by the nation's businesses.

It may be that the growth and decline of the economies of city and state are positively correlated with the influx of Navajos to Albuquerque. The greatest period of Albuquerque's economic growth was the decade 1950–60. In these ten years, 111 Navajos moved to Albuquerque, a larger number than for any other comparable period in the city's history.

As has been previously noted, Albuquerque experienced an impressive postwar expansion of the population. In 1946 the population was 50,000. By 1960 federal census results showed that it had increased to 201,189. Of this total 195,264 were classed as Anglo, 3,568 as Negro, approximately 1,800 as Indian, 42,947 as "White, Spanish Surname: Native," and 2,357 as "other races." It is interesting to note the city's Indian population in 1950 was 2,233; thus there was a decrease in this category between 1950 and 1960. The city's population as a whole, however, increased 107.8 per cent, most of this increment being in the Anglo resident category. The fact that the Albuquerque Navajo population increased during this decade while that of Indians other than Navajo decreased is of some interest, although the significance of this change is not readily evident.

A report of the New Mexico State Employment Service Research Unit (1961) provides a limited source of information on worker migration in Albuquerque. The data are supplied by "persons registering in the Albuquerque Offices of the New Mexico State Employment Service during the April 26th to May 25th, 1960, period" (1). The study attempts to show the amount and direction of migration and the educational and occupational characteristics of certain defined groups of workers.

During the period under consideration, this agency processed 963 individuals. Five categories of workers were studied:

1. *Local Worker* — One who lives in New Mexico, started work in New Mexico, and whose last job was in New Mexico; 2. *Local-Return Worker* — One who lives in New Mexico, started work in New Mexico, and whose last job was outside New Mexico; 3. *Local In-Migrant Worker* — One who lives in New Mexico, started work outside New Mexico, and whose last job was in New Mexico; 4. *In-Migrant Worker* — One who lives in New Mexico, started work outside New Mexico, and whose last job was outside New Mexico; 5. *Tran-*

sient — One who lives outside New Mexico or who has no permanent address (1-2).

The conclusions of the study are summarized (33–9) as follows:

While it was found that 50 per cent of the registrants had originated in New Mexico, it was also found that 50 per cent . . . were the result of migration . . . this would tend to indicate the area's dependence upon other states for its worker supply. . . . Local Workers made their most significant contribution to the service, unskilled and entry occupants. Local-Return Workers were (found evenly distributed in all seven occupational groups, i.e. professional and managerial, clerical and sales, service, agriculture, skilled, semi-skilled, and unskilled). . . . Local In-Migrants were heavy contributors to the professional-managerial and skilled occupations. In-Migrant Workers were fairly well distributed over the various occupations with the exception of being somewhat low in the unskilled categories. Transient Workers were predominantly in the unskilled categories and contributed very little to any occupational group. . . . The sex composition of Local Workers and Local In-Migrants was in equal percentage distribution. Most noticeable variations occurred in the Local-Return and Transient Groups where males predominated. In the case of Local-Return Workers, this probably is the result of heads of families returning home after employment elsewhere. The Transient composition, being all male, is what would normally be expected from a mobile group composed of persons without family ties or workers leaving their families for a 'work-search' effort. The highest percentage of females were represented by the In-Migrants which could possibly be accounted for by wives of service personnel in the area. . . . The Local Worker groups had the lowest percentage of workers in the prime working years of 21 to 44 years of age, but contained the highest percentage of workers under 21, which could normally be expected. . . . Local-Return Workers were composed predominantly of workers between the ages of 21 and 44. . . . While Local In-Migrants, In-Migrants and Transients exhibited a higher percentage of workers between 21 and 44 years of age than did the Local Worker group, they also contributed a higher percentage of workers 45 years and over . . . it was found that the group possessing the highest amount of education (a high school diploma) was the Local-Return group. This may be an indication that the higher educated Local Workers leave the area . . . the Local Workers who left the area and returned exhibit a higher level of education than the Local Workers who remained and higher than groups moving in from other areas of origin. Local Workers had the lowest degree of education. The number of Local In-Migrant Workers with four years high school or more of education exceeded the Local group by some 11 per cent. The workers who were currently moving into the area had 9 per cent more of their number with four years high school or more than the

group which previously migrated into the area and 20 per cent more than the Local group . . . It would appear that unemployment in the state of last employment had some bearing upon the return of Local Workers to their area of origin. . . . There does not seem to be an established relationship between unemployment rates and movement of the In-Migrant Worker group . . . the mobility of (transients) appeared to be more individual in its basis than as a result of unemployment in the area of the last job. . . .

If the unwarranted assumption were made that these data are representative of non-Navajo Albuquerque migrants, Navajo migrants would resemble non-Navajo migrants to Albuquerque in that they are in the same age range, twenty to forty. They would differ from them in that they are much fewer in number and their migration rate is lower, as is their general level of education. Navajo migrants appear to resemble the non-Navajo "Local-Worker" category.

The corporate limits of Albuquerque encompass an area of fifty-nine square miles (see Fig. 3). The city is roughly divided into quadrants by Central Avenue which runs east and west and the Santa Fe Railway tracks which run north and south. Outside the city limits, but still an integral part of Albuquerque are the "north and south valleys," each extending about five miles along the east bank of the Rio Grande River. These two areas consist of homes, small businesses, and farms. The farms are limited in size because of the scant amounts of water available for irrigation. At least one-third of this land is dry, treeless, and unoccupied. The city has a small "downtown" decaying business section which is being supplanted by shopping centers in the northwest and northeast suburbs.

Albuquerque's "Skid Row" is a rectangular area south of Central Street on either side of the railroad station, extending about four blocks on a north-south axis and ten blocks on an east-west axis. Skid Row consists of a few shabby taverns, liquor stores, flop houses, and missions. Much of the taverns' regular trade consists of prostitutes, pimps, and their clients. Most residents of the city refer to this section as "First Street." The area southeast of Skid Row—west of South Broadway to the river and east to Maple Street—is occupied predominately by Negroes, although many Spanish-speaking people live here.

The newest and "most desirable" section of the city is the "Northeast Heights" where many professional and prosperous businessmen live with their families. There seems to be little evidence of discrimination in housing, except toward some Negroes. Spanish-speaking, Anglo, and Indian residents live where they can afford to rent or buy. There are several areas in the northwest, southwest, and southeast quadrants of the city whose residents are largely "Spanish," Negro, and Indian, but this settlement pattern is due for the most part to income and not to discrimination.

NON-NAVAJO ALBUQUERQUE INDIANS

The Indian residents of Albuquerque have always been inconspicuous occupants of the city. Most non-Indians are unaware of their presence and the majority even deny that Indians live here. Because of my restricted research interests and a lack of time, I was able to learn very little regarding non-Navajo Indians living in Albuquerque. It seems reasonable to assume that Indians have lived in town throughout its history. Stanley (1963: 16) mentions that 603 Indians were living in "Albuquerque and vicinity" in 1784. The first non-Navajo Indian resident in this century that I knew about was a Hopi who lived and worked as a silversmith near the Santa Fe Railway station about 1910. He made yearly trips to his home on Third Mesa. A retired missionary informant characterized him as a congenial but somewhat shy individual. While on a visit to the Hopi reservation in the early 1930's he contracted pneumonia and died.

It was estimated in 1927 that there were 100 Indian residents in Albuquerque (Meriam 1928: 706). Thirty-four Indians were contacted: twenty-seven Pueblo, four Navajos, two Hopi, and one Apache. The researchers found that there was no "Indian quarter." "The families are scattered about, generally comparatively remote from each other. The houses themselves can seldom be criticised on grounds of insanitation or insufficiency" (707). The Indians lived "in cheaper working class neighborhoods" (707). Nineteen men (708) were working at the following occupations: three clerks or salesmen; two truckers; three domestic or restaurant workers; five railroad employees; one janitor; two silversmiths; one printer; one lineman for a telephone company; and one farmer. Some of these people were Navajos, but occupations are not given by tribe.

A number of miscellaneous data are provided. Hospitality was not extended to kinsmen and friends. Employers regarded Indians as satisfactory employees. Recreation and dietary habits resembled those of the Anglo population. Married women did not take jobs. Indian students at the University and the city's public schools did satisfactory work (713). Indians "return for ceremonials to their respective pueblos and reservations less often than do the Indians at Winslow and Gallup."

A retired missionary told me that he and his wife organized an "All-Indian Club" which existed during the period 1932–34. Meetings were held in the YMCA which was located near the railroad station. The club was formed because "there were many good young Indians in town who had no entertainment." The missionary ran the club because the Indian members "just didn't know how to run things." Sixteen different tribes were represented, and the usual attendance ranged between thirty and forty. Generally the entertainment consisted of "readings and pantomimes." The club broke up because of a feud between the superintendent of the Albuquerque Indian School and another clergyman who was also a sponsor. My missionary informant also stated that he and his wife "got tired of doing all the work," which may have been the crucial factor in the club's demise.

White (1962: 67–78) discusses the conversion of a few residents of Zia to a "Holy Roller" Negro church in Albuquerque in the late 1920's. These converts were driven out of the pueblo and some of them lived in town for a while during the 1930's.

Hawley (1948: 15) was exceedingly pessimistic about the Pueblo Indians' ability to have a satisfying life in Albuquerque.

The majority of the Pueblo Indians today, if moved into Albuquerque, and dropped upon the city limits, one year or five years later would be found still upon the outskirts, living as day laborers, under conditions of poor housing and poor sanitation, their neighbors the lower class Whites (often among the least tolerant of Americans), and their comments upon life tinged with the bitterness of not being able to attain such luxuries of life as they admire around them or such unity with the community as may insure a feeling of self respect and self importance. They would be held in this position by the relative lack of higher education within their mass as well as by related financial problems, but their children would have the advantage of city schools and the association with non-Indian children. Such association would, however, be broken to a considerable extent, just as contacts in adult community life are limited or broken by the ethnic or 'race' prejudices unfortunately so common to American people as a whole.

The non-Navajo Albuquerque Indians during the period 1959–61 could be divided into three general categories: (1) the professional Indians; (2) the "permanent residents" who worked at more or less conventional jobs; and (3) the pueblo commuters.

"Chief Grey Eagle" and his family — professionals — danced for tourists at Old Town during most of the year. They were originally from Jemez where they were regarded as undesirable by both liberal and conservative factions. The reasons for this attitude are unknown. When dancing, these Indians wore neo-plains type costumes.

The "Turquoise Dancers" consisted of about twelve people who also wore neo-plains type garb when dancing. In January, 1961, they danced for the opening of a new bank building in downtown Albuquerque. The tribal identity of these people is not known.

In the spring of 1961 near the plush Western Skies Motel on the east side of town near Highway 66, the "First American Indian Land Amusement Park" was being built. Part of this complex was to consist of a "village" with Apache, Navajo, Pueblo, Sioux, and Ute Indians on display. A brochure describes their activities:

The five tribes of First American Indian Land will perform for your pleasure. World famous for their colorful costumes and intricate dances, these Indians will enchant you with their descriptive pantomimes. Dances for war, rain, crops and a successful hunt — all are part of their ritual. Hoop and fertility dances carry special significance. . . .

I know nothing of the activities of these Indians. A Jicarilla boy was selected to play the part of a comic strip character "Little Beaver."

A professional Indian of a different sort was a very talented woman painter from Santa Clara. She had had several successful showings throughout the Southwest and was in demand as a speaker by many local women's clubs.

In Albuquerque, at the time of my work, there were at least 200 Laguna Indians who were collectively known as "The Laguna Colony." Like other Indian residents they were scattered throughout the city. They were required to attend Laguna Club meetings and were fined if they did not appear. With the exception of non-Laguna spouses, these meetings were restricted to members of this pueblo. According to one informant, these Indians maintained homes in town and at the pueblo. Most pueblo ceremonies were attended and often participated in.

Lange (1959: 189) states that in 1948, nineteen people from Cochiti lived in Albuquerque. In 1959 I knew of two Cochiti Indians working as silversmiths in Old Town.

About 100 Indians from the area worked as silversmiths at such places as Bells and Maisels, at wages of less than $1.00 per hour. Some of these were Pueblo and a few were Navajo.

There were five organizations that catered exclusively to all Indians in the city: the Council of American Indians, the Lamanite Chapter of the Church of Jesus Christ of Latter-day Saints, two other church groups, and the Turquoise Lodge. The Council was organized by a small number of prosperous Indians in the early part of 1960. Its goals were ambitious but comfortably vague: "to promote the welfare of the American Indian in the home, school, church, and the community." This club prided itself on having a membership restricted to Indians who are "people who think and are willing to work to get things done." Six months after its origin, it had sixteen members, nine of whom were officers. A year later it boasted between fifty and sixty members. One Navajo belonged and other groups represented were San Carlos Apache, Creek, San Felipe, Santo Domingo, and Laguna. This club may or may not have been as dynamic as its members claimed.

The Lamanite Chapter of the Mormon Church was led by a former resident of Acoma, Henry Davis, who was married to a woman who said that she was "one-eighth Laguna." Davis, along with his brother and father, worked as a professional Indian in a circus which toured Europe during the years 1926–28. Shortly after this time, his family was driven out of the pueblo because his father had refused to permit his children to be initiated into the appropriate societies. He felt that since they had embraced Christianity such action would be inappropriate. Davis had lived in Albuquerque since that time and had on at least two occasions acted as an informant for anthropologists. At the time I knew him, he was running a shabby motel on East Central Street. He said that the Lamanite Chapter had about ninety members. None of these were Navajo.

One of the Baptist churches in town encouraged Indians to attend its functions and gave some instructions in reading and writing English. An interdenominational "Christian Indian Mission" directed its activities mainly toward the Indian school students. Its pastor felt that the work had not been too successful to date.

The Turquoise Lodge is a sanatorium for Indian alcoholics. I knew nothing about its activities.

Residents of Isleta, Sandia, and Jemez work in town during the day and return to their pueblos each night. Isleta is only 25 minutes by car from Albuquerque. Informants have estimated that at least 75 per cent of the adults here have either full or part-time jobs in Albuquerque. Isleta is also the major source for the city's Indian prostitutes. There are probably not more than fifty Indian women working at this trade since most of the demand is for Anglo women. Sandia is perhaps closer to Albuquerque, but I have no details of its residents' city activities. Jemez is about an hour away from town by car. Many of the women from here work as domestics. Their daily routine is long and demanding. They normally leave Jemez at 6:00 a.m. and return around 7:00 or 8:00 p.m. Their transportation is usually provided by those of the pueblo who own pick-up trucks and charge $2.00 a day for a round trip. Ceremonial obligations prevent most Jemez men from holding jobs in town.

I know of two men, one from Santo Domingo and the other from San Felipe, who held semi-skilled but reasonably well-paying jobs at Sandia Corporation. The religious officials at their pueblos asked them to assume ceremonial offices which would require their full-time residence in their villages for at least a year. If they refused to accept these positions, they and their immediate families would be permanently expelled from the pueblos. They quit their jobs in the city and returned home. It is my impression that most adult pueblo men who live at a pueblo or reasonably close to it are "requested" to take similar positions at least once every three or four years.

This study does not consider Indian boarding school students (800 to 1,000 Navajos), who are currently at the Albuquerque Indian School and the Nazarene Bible School, or the Indian patients (100), who are at the various tuberculosis sanatoriums and the Bernalillo County Indian Hospital.

THE HISTORY OF NAVAJOS IN ALBUQUERQUE

It is difficult to reconstruct the history of the Navajo presence in Albuquerque because of a dearth of written records and suitable informants. During their 75-year residence (1887–1961), most Navajo Indians have lived in Albuquerque virtually unnoticed. Only the more lurid details of the earlier residents' lives have come to light. The ordinary or "normal" aspects of their urban existence generally have been forgotten.

An understanding of the operation of the Albuquerque Indian School (AIS) is important because it seems that, while a few Indians came to adopt permanent urban residence because of their stay there, many were driven back to the reservations, too disgusted by their exposure to this version of Anglo ways to consider adopting them permanently. The AIS and others like it have played very minor roles in the early urbanization of Navajos because most Navajo parents were reluctant to send their children to school until just prior to World War II. They felt that they would be "happier" and more useful as sheep herders on the reservation.

Those Navajos and other Indian students who did enroll found school life somewhat arduous. They were given free room, board, and clothing but had to sign three-year "contracts" stating that they would agree to remain at the School for that period. The School was run on a rigid military basis, and many of the instructors were former Army officers. All boys wore uniforms and were subjected to intensive drills and inspections.

Prior to 1932, the majority of the student body was allowed "to go to town" once a year. A few of the brightest students were permitted to attend a local high school for their junior and senior years since instruction at this level was not offered at the Indian School until 1925. Any unauthorized off-campus trips were regarded as "desertion," and offenders usually spent two weeks in the guard house. Until it was torn down by government order in 1929, the guard house was a rather grim and unwholesome place. The 1928 report on Indian administration describes this establishment (Meriam: 332-3):

At Albuquerque attention was drawn to a structure closely resembling a Mexican hut. Closer observation revealed a solid concrete, box-like building, with a door and one small window. It was barely large enough to accommodate two iron beds and a small stove. Otherwise it was devoid of furnishings. It was surrounded by a barricade of heavy wire and miscellaneous boards woven into a high fence. The grounds surrounding this unit were untidy and the interior was dirty. There were no toilet facilities or running water.

McKinney (1934: 92–3) concludes that the passing of the guard house had a bad effect on AIS discipline:

. . . discipline became lax and disorder and desertions increased greatly. During this year (1928–1929) fifty-one boys deserted. Reuben Perry (the school principal) said 'It is a sad commentary to have to state that more of our pupils have been in the city and county jails during the last twenty months than had been in the school guardhouse for a number of years . . . about this time the paddling of boys on the naked flesh with the rubber sole of a hospital slipper became frowned upon.

A normal school day began at 4:00 a.m. and ended at 8:00 or 9:00 p.m. Emphasis was placed on "agricultural, mechanical and domestic skills." In effect, this meant that to the greatest possible extent students were responsible for the repair and maintenance of the school's physical plant. Those students having a good academic standing were appointed "assistants" and paid a very nominal salary. The "assistant farmer" cleaned out the dairy and horse barns, the "assistant engineer" kept the boilers fired during the cooler months, and the "assistant cooks" did menial kitchen labor.

Pueblo and Navajo students were encouraged to join the Hiawatha and Minnehaha Dramatic Society. If this did not appeal to them, they could become members of the debate club and argue such burning issues as "Resolved: That Indians should not be encouraged to have more than six years of education." Sports, such as track, football, and baseball, were enjoyed by almost all the boys, and "shop" was the most popular subject.

Great efforts were made to induce students to abandon their cultural heritage. Those speaking their native languages on campus who were capable of speaking English were subject to severe penalties. Students were discouraged from returning to their reservations when school was not in session, instead being urged to go on "outing"; that is, to take a temporary or part-time job away from the reservation and off-campus. The outing system was started in about 1902 or 1903 and continued until the Collier administration, which began in 1933. McKinney describes the activities of some of the AIS students in this program about 1902.

At various times of the year there were sixty-six boys and eight girls on outings. Fifty-two boys were sent to the beet fields at Rocky Ford, Colorado, while the remainder worked on the railroad, or for local farmers. The girls worked as domestics. The total net earnings for these children was $2350. During the year seventeen girls worked for families in Albuquerque and earned from $10 to $15 a month. It was impossible to supply the demand for this kind of help.

The students, of course, were allowed to keep the money that they had earned. Despite this and other benefits, many did not seem to enjoy campus life. McKinney (70) comments regarding the school year 1916–17, "there were no serious infractions of discipline during the year but sixty boys deserted." Poor health conditions also contributed to student dissatisfaction. Tuberculosis, diphtheria, typhoid, and smallpox took a heavy toll on the student body, and today the school can boast of a well-filled but abandoned cemetery.

Students who were able to desert, return to the reservation, and avoid the BIA police sent after them were accorded great prestige by their kinsmen and friends. The farther the distance necessary to travel to return, the greater prestige attached to the feat. Since students had to walk unassisted between 200 to 300 miles to reach home, successful desertion was a respectable accomplishment.

Most students returned to the reservation within four or five years. A few, however, became permanent residents off the reservation.

Additional data relevant to Navajo history in Albuquerque will be presented chronologically. However, this chronological order will be ignored where the extent of data and the demands of effective prose require it. All individuals mentioned by name are Navajo but with the exception of Marshall Tome and Elle Ganado, the names of all Indians are fictitious.

1881. The Albuquerque Indian School began. Buildings were leased from the Presbyterian Church and soon after were purchased by the government.

1887. There were eight Navajo students at AIS. Most of these came from the Checkerboard area. They spoke little or no English and consequently their education was highly elementary.

1893. Sam Jones was an assistant engineer at AIS.

1894. Jim Williams was hired as a laborer at AIS. Sam Jones was still working in the same capacity, but at a lower salary. This reduction in pay was due to drunken behavior. George James was hired as a laborer.

1899. Mary Johnson was the first Navajo student to die of consumption and be buried in the school cemetery. An attendance record book, dated at this time, has the following entry: "[illegible], a Navajo, ran away for thirty days with a female Navajo student. He returned with her, was married the next day and expelled."

1901–02. Seven Indian employees were working at AIS. These were not students. Health conditions were extremely poor.

1903. A rather exciting incident occurred at a "State Fair" in Albuquerque. An Army officer brought in twenty-five Navajos from the Torreon area to take part in a mock battle with a local detachment of United States Cavalry. The Navajos felt that the dramatic effect would be heightened if live ammunition was substituted just prior to the performance. No casualties occurred on either side, but all spectators abruptly left the stands. Jim Williams acted as an interpreter for the event. There were 348 Navajo students at AIS. Robert, age thirty-one, was a private in the police force. Joe Humphrey from Canyoncito worked as a campus policeman for thirty days.

1904. McKinney (1934: 42) characterizes the Navajos as students:

Of the 336 Navajos enrolled, 313 were full blood. Progress in school was fair. About 60 per cent of the students were unable to speak or understand English. With the exception of a small class of older pupils, the entire school was primary; however, a fine quality of workmanship was shown in the handicrafts.

1905. Mildred Harris "from Canyoncito, age twenty-one," was an assistant cook.

1906. A Navajo "leader" from Canyoncito was induced to "appeal" for statehood for the territory before a traveling Congressional Committee. Jim Williams acted as interpreter, and was still working as a laborer at AIS. Frank Roberts was a private in the school police force and Robert, too, was still working as a policeman. Paul Adams was a farmer.

1907. Hoot Prince enrolled as a student. Other Navajo students who were there at this time were John Smith, Red Jenson, Willard Harrison, Martin Andrews, and Merton Ford. Jim Williams and Paul Adams were still there in the same capacities. Jim Williams was not married and now lived in a second floor apartment on the corner of Second and Iron Streets. During this time, the few Navajo residents of Albuquerque kept to themselves and had little to do with Anglos or Spanish-speaking people. This self-imposed isolation was partially due to language

barriers, and the effects of the stories which these Navajos had been told by their elders about the Long Walk, and the cruelty and general unworthiness of Anglos.

1908. Hening and Johnson (1908: 24) make the earliest reference to hogans within the city limits: A group of skilled Navajo weavers, basketmakers, and silversmiths are kept busy in the Fred Harvey Museum and curio rooms, where the finest collection of the arts and crafts of the Indians in the west is replenished constantly with fresh products from the reservation. . . . Blanketed Indians ride in trolley cars; a village of Navajo "hogans" nestles near three-story business blocks.

These hogans were located near the YMCA on North First Street within two blocks of the railroad station. Informants disagree as to their number, with estimates varying from three to six. It is probable that prior to World War I there were five or six, and that the number decreased to two or three in 1935 when these remaining structures were torn down.

There were not more than six or eight Navajos living here at one time. The Fred Harvey Company hired these Indians to work as weavers and silversmiths. They were also expected to sit glumly under the shade of the train station roof whenever transcontinental passenger trains came through. Apparently the Railway and the Company felt that passengers would be entertained by such antics.

These Navajos divided their residence between Albuquerque and the reservation, usually close to Ganado. The Indians felt that they always had to return to the reservation when a relative died or was sick. George Evans, the Navajos' Anglo supervisor, said that he could not determine just how his employees knew about the death or illness of a reservation kinsman, but they frequently came to him with such a story and asked for a railroad pass. He always gave them one. Much of this misfortune was most probably fictitious. The Navajos simply wanted to go back to the reservation for a time. Silversmiths employed by the company were Tom Wallace, "a big tall man;" Mike Whitehouse; Big George; David Nelson; Harry Bennett; and Willie (?).

Their best weaver was a woman known as Elle of Ganado or Elle Ganado. Elle, with her husband Clyde, came to work for the Company in 1915. She died near Ganado about 1927. Huckel (1928: 15) describes her as an excellent weaver who was very popular with tourists. A Fred Harvey post card (1921, No. 10936) supplies the following data:

Clyde of Ganado is the husband of Elle, the most famous weaver among the Navajos, and shares with her to a great extent her fame and popularity. Both of them are perhaps the most widely known of all their tribe. There is a romance connected with his marriage to Elle, the substance of which is that he stole her from her mother's hogan and carried her off on his pony at night. He is an interesting study and a born story teller.

Two informants agreed that Clyde was either a "medicine man" or a singer because he was always collecting various herbs, plants, and grasses in and around town.

Evans stated that Elle had no children but considered herself to be a "mother" to all other Navajos in town. A Navajo informant said that Elle had two daughters who carded wool for her and also did some weaving. Jack Holt, a Navajo student who left AIS because of a poor academic standing, married one of her daughters in 1917. When she died, he married her younger sister. Both daughters lacked formal schooling. Holt did not live with his wife's kin, but moved into an adobe building near the corner of Seventh and Tijeras NW Streets. For a few years he worked for a wholesale clothing house and the Grunsfeld Company.

Martha Johns and her daughter Harriet Joe worked as weavers for Fred Harvey in 1929.

Clyde Ganado worked as a janitor at the Company and spoke English well. Elle understood English but never attempted to speak it. The Company treated these people well and supplied them with meat, coffee, coal, and potatoes. The smiths and weavers were paid by the piece and received such reimbursement as 25c for a silver button, 35c for a button with wire and silver balls, and 50c for a bracelet. The Navajos stole small amounts of silver and turquoise occasionally, but Evans raised no serious objections to this practice. At their request, they were paid in Mexican silver dollars which they could either spend or make into jewelry.

Those who knew of these Navajos said that they were congenial but lacked formal schooling and showed little or no interest in the surrounding city life. Other Navajos from the reservation often visited them. One informant told me that those Anglos living close to the hogans found the occasional public "cootie hunts," or lice-picking sessions, of the Navajos to be disconcerting. Surplus livestock frequently invaded the nearby YMCA.

In 1935 the Company stopped hiring Navajo silversmiths and weavers because it was losing money on the rug and jewelry concessions. The former Navajo employees returned permanently to the reservation and the hogans were torn down.

My sources agree that there was another group of hogans occupied by Navajos near a railroad viaduct adjacent to the corner of Broadway and Central Street. It is not known how many Navajos lived here, when they came, or when they abandoned the hogans. They had disappeared by 1930. Apparently a few Navajos lived here who were rather poor silversmiths. A retired dealer in Indian goods said that the hogans were occupied only for brief periods of time and that the smiths who lived in them had lived and worked at other places off the reservation such as Denver, New York, and Washington, D.C.

In 1908 Philip Brown was still working for the school police force. Tony Brown, age seventeen, came to AIS as a student from Cabezon, New Mexico. Brown gained a certain notoriety in May, 1919, when he was beaten to death by "a person or persons unknown." When he had left the school in 1916, he had worked for the Santa Fe shops in Albuquerque as a "handy man" and then served in the Army for about one year.

1909–19. During this period the following Navajo students attended AIS: Douglas Wolf, Foster Prince ("half-brother" of Hoot Prince), Ed Nelson, Herbert Wilson, Howard George, Andy Willis, Ross Wills, Fred Marx, Eddie Roberts, Mark Henry, Matthew Brace, Helen Blackwood, Margaret Gibbs, Marvin Radcliffe, and Luke Stein. There were, of course, many other Navajos in school, but these names appear in the few surviving records. All of these individuals came from the eastern portion of Navajo country, or, if a straight line were drawn from Dinnehotso to Holbrook, most of the Navajo students and residents would have come from east of this line.

Most of these students returned to the reservation. Some came to an unhappy end. Marvin Radcliffe was killed in a car accident. Fred Marx committed suicide shortly after returning to the reservation in 1922. Foster Prince was injured while doing carpentry work and spent the rest of his life as a cripple. Andy Willis became a good carpenter and married a woman at Isleta Pueblo. When she died in 1925, he became a chronic alcoholic. Luke Stein is one of the finest silversmiths in the country, but is also an alcoholic.

Some lived better. Helen Blackwood eventually became a public school teacher. She was also one of the few Navajos who genuinely embraced Christianity. It is suspected that her principal reason for not returning to the reservation was the fact that her immediate family and other relatives died in a flu epidemic. Missionaries had reared her until she was sixteen when she was enrolled at AIS.

Hoot Prince served over a year in the Army as an athlete and a horseshoer. He worked for the Santa Fe as a machinist and then as an inspector for many years. With the exception of a first unhappy marriage, he led a reasonably normal urban existence. He also stayed in the city because there was nothing for him on the reservation. His stepfather literally drove him out of the family hogan and his other relatives regarded him only as an inexhaustible source of menial labor.

Margaret Gibbs graduated from the Albuquerque High School, worked as a domestic in town for a few years, and then returned to her home at Fort Defiance. Presumably the others also returned to the reservation. My informants could tell me nothing about them after they left AIS. Most did not complete the ten years of training then available.

1920–46. The following Navajos became Albuquerque residents during this period: Joe and Minnie Short, Bill White, Paul and Betty Long, Dave Ellis, Sr., Bob Elliot, Rhoda Silver, Rod Fields, Tom Jefferson, Roger Ball, and Burt Harrison. Hoot Prince married Abby Seaton of Isleta Pueblo. Betty Long, who had an Anglo father, married Howard Hopkinson, a Zuni. Paul Long married an Anglo woman and worked in a local newspaper's printing shop. Betty stated that the Navajos regarded her as an Anglo because she could not speak Navajo and the Anglos regarded her as a Navajo because her mother was a Navajo. She stated that she could live like an Anglo or Navajo, but would stay in town because of her children. Her brother spoke some Navajo, but looked like an Anglo. The brother and sister and their families were virtually isolated.

Rod Fields and Tom Jefferson were AIS students who stayed in town. Both worked as carpenters on an independent basis. They did not marry, and returned to the reservation after three years in Albuquerque. In 1920 Tom Jefferson was working as a janitor at a reservation Catholic Mission. In 1928 a company called Maisels began hiring Navajos as silversmiths. Luke Stein was given a job as shop manager. He created the first designs to be used in the machine production of "Indian" tourist jewelry. From this time until the beginning of World War II a large number of Navajo and Pueblo Indians worked as smiths for this firm. Because of the low pay and other possible unknown factors, they all stayed a short time and then moved to another urban area or back to the reservation.

During the school year 1928–29, 287 students were enrolled at AIS. In 1929 Bill White came to Albuquerque and worked at Maisels. Until he was drafted at the beginning of World War II, he supported himself by working as a silversmith and a manual laborer. In 1961, I learned that he had married a woman from San Juan Pueblo and was living there. He worked on construction jobs and farmed. In 1932, thirty-seven Navajos received high school diplomas from AIS. In 1933 Sam Jackson and Dave Elliot, Sr., worked in the AIS carpenter shop. Sam Jackson did not return to the reservation but worked at various construction jobs in the Southwest until he died of cancer in Albuquerque in 1946. Dave Elliot, Sr., did the same kind of work, but returned to the reservation in the 1950's to work for the tribe. He was fired for stealing building materials and returned to Albuquerque to work as a carpenter. For the last twelve years he has been active in anti-tribal administration movements. He married a Navajo woman and presently owns his own home in Albuquerque where he is employed at AIS as a carpenter.

In 1933, Tylor Jefferson, the uncle of Tom Jefferson, came to town from Fort Defiance to "retire." He came here because "his sisters-in-law" were interested in him. Jefferson died in Albuquerque in about 1957.

Burt Harrison came to Albuquerque during 1933 to be employed as a silversmith. He did not return to the reservation, probably because he had had no real home there. His mother had been a prostitute who had lived in the reservation border towns and Albuquerque. An elderly Navajo woman who knew his mother found him abandoned. He served in the Marines and returned to Albuquerque immediately after the War where he worked as a shop manager at Maisels and at Bells, where he is currently employed. He married the sister of Henry Davis, the Acoma Mormon.

In 1935, Roger Ball walked from his home in Sanders, Arizona, to Albuquerque, a distance of about 275 miles. He was allowed to take a six months' course in silversmithing at AIS. He then followed this trade and worked on various construction jobs until he was drafted in 1942. About this time, John Collier's infamous stock reduction program was making its weight felt throughout the reservation. Many Navajo stockmen, especially the owners of small herds, were left destitute with so few sheep and cattle that they could not support their families by their former means of livelihood. Ball's family was in this category. His activities during the period 1935–46 are representative of many young unmarried Navajos of that time. Within a period of two years, Ball had worked as a silversmith in Albuquerque, Cerillos, Santa Fe, and Colorado. In 1936 he worked as a smith in Tulsa and then got a job as a roughneck in the oil fields of West Texas. Silversmithing is generally a seasonal business and smiths are often employed only until enough goods are accumulated to meet the demands of the Christmas and summer tourist seasons. Since the only other "skill" a Navajo smith usually has is manual labor, which sometimes pays less than smithing, he can do nothing but take part-time work and migrate to where employment opportunities temporarily exist.

In 1936, the Collier administration, by "rearranging the budget" made it almost impossible for Navajo students to go to AIS for high school training. Those who wanted to go to high school had to apply to the single school open to them, Fort Wingate. However, a very few Navajos were admitted at Albuquerque if they were able to give the United Pueblo Agency Superintendent "a sad enough story." This policy continued until after World War II. Franklin Johnson was one of the few Navajo students enrolled at AIS then.

Little is known about Albuquerque Navajo activities during World War II because most of my Navajo informants were in the service and stationed outside the Southwest. Dave Taft from Coolidge worked for the Santa Fe about this time, but he soon grew tired of the work and went back to being a professional Indian. He had also had an unfortunate "affair" with an Anglo woman and felt that it was to his advantage to leave town. He, along with several others, toured various elementary schools throughout the country.

I know of only three Navajos who came to Albuquerque during the War to work. It may well be that with the tremendously increased demands for laborers during this time and higher pay scales for seasonal labor it was possible for many Navajos to live on the reservation and yet make an adequate salary from seasonal work.

1946–61. During this time 180 of the current

(1961) Navajo residents of Albuquerque came to town. Ninety-six came during the period 1946–50. Forty-five more came in the years 1956–57.

In 1946 many Navajos came to Albuquerque who otherwise would not have because of an assistance program encompassed in the "GI Bill" or the Servicemen's Readjustment Act. This program was known to local veterans as the "52-20 Club," because an unemployed veteran could collect payments of $20 a week for a year. But in order to be eligible, a Navajo veteran had to move off the reservation. Hench, many Navajos came to Albuquerque just to get these unemployment checks. Albuquerque was preferable to Gallup or Farmington because the Veterans Administration (VA) offices in those cities became aware of the fact that Navajos in their area were taking an unfair advantage of the situation. They came to town only to collect their checks and continued to live unemployed on the reservation, and soon it became almost impossible for a Navajo to receive this compensation in these two places. The following Navajos, living in Albuquerque in 1961, first came because of this inducement: Barney Prescott, Nelson Adams, Walter Higgins, Basil Evans, Morris Charles, Jim Frazer, Mike Frazer, Henry Chavez, Louis Goodwin, Milt Chase, Charlie Davidson, Wilbur Manners, Willy Perry, Irving Cohen, Tom John, and Mark Jennings.

A Navajo informant who worked for the VA in helping administer this program estimated that there were about 42 Navajos in town in 1946 collecting this money. Of this total, 20 stayed in Albuquerque permanently, and 22 went back to the reservation at the end of the year. Some of those who returned were maladjusted drunks, but many were not. Ted Singer is now a respected tribal councilman. Dan Jones is an administrative assistant for the tribe at Window Rock.

In 1948 Julius Goldman built two dome-type hogans behind his curio shop near the corner of Lomas and Central as living quarters for his silversmiths and their families. Building these hogans was Goldman's idea but his employees were willing enough to live in them. The Navajos were originally from St. Michaels and Canyoncito. Many drank to excess and often fought while drunk. They were Ruddy Suggs and his wife Flora; Robert Suggs (the son of Ruddy) and his wife; Larry Dent and his wife Marlene; Ruthie, Ruddy's sometime married daughter; an unmarried male Navajo, possibly Ambrose Nelson; and Pete Charles and his wife. Marlene Dent ran off with a "Mexican" and married him. Larry Dent then married another Navajo, but did not live in the hogans long. Ruthie had two children by an Anglo husband and killed one of them by falling on it when she was drunk. Her husband robbed Goldman's store of $2,000 worth of jewelry and was sent to the state penitentiary for a few years.

These people were paid by the hour. Ruddy received $1.20 an hour and his son Robert, $1.10 because "he drank more than his father." Presents were given to the Navajos only at Christmas time. They consisted of food.

These Navajos had frequent visitors from the reservation. Ruddy often hired singers to come and conduct sings. Goldman didn't know what these chants were, but he did remember on one occasion seeing the singer stuff "bamboo grass and herbs" into a hollow tube. The visits by singers began as soon as the hogans were built and continued until they were torn down in 1955.

Apparently Pete Charles and his wife moved into the hogan vacated by Larry Dent. Charles was very dangerous when he was drunk. His Navajo wife left him after he smashed in one side of her face by dropping the lid of a car trunk on her. Pete's brother Tom was nearly killed one night in a drunken brawl at the hogans.

The two hogans were torn down at the insistence of the Public Health Department because they were too dirty. This office told Goldman that if he wanted to keep them, he would have to install flush toilets. He refused to do this because his Navajo tenants would have had no respect for such machinery.

The Suggs family moved to a single room dwelling near the western city limits, where they were at the time of this study. Their general behavior patterns have remained the same. When the weather permits and she is sober, Flora sets up a vertical loom behind the house and weaves poor quality rugs. The family prefers to eat outside around a fire rather than use a wood stove in the kitchen. Ruddy often beats his wife and daughter-in-law when he is drunk. Robert, in a moment of drunken confusion, drank a bottle of concentrated nitric acid which he normally used in his smithing. He seems to have recovered. Ruthie has had two "illegitimate children" by Ambrose Nelson. This affair may have been occasioned by her husband's long term in jail. Pete Charles came under the influence of one of the local Baptist churches, stopped drinking, and married another Navajo woman.

All these people still work as silversmiths but sometimes pick piñon nuts in the slack season. Ruddy once told me that he and his family left St. Michaels because he claimed the Catholics "stole" his land. They then moved to Canyoncito, but found life equally unsatisfactory there. Finally they came to Albuquerque. When possible, they live with friends and kinsmen at Canyoncito and the St. Michaels area.

The Special Five Year Navajo Educational Program began in 1946, and in 1948, according to Young (1961: 44), started at AIS. This Program is an attempt to train large numbers of Navajo adolescents who have had little or no formal schooling and have no knowledge of the dimensions and requirements of off-reservation living. For the first three years, these students ideally acquire some facility in speaking, reading, and writing English, accept improved health practices, and become able to cope adequately with most Anglo customs and manners. During the last two years training is divided equally between general elementary academic work and learning a "vocation" which will enable students to be economically independent off the reservation. Such jobs as baby-sitting, menial kitchen work, and construction labor are regarded as vocations. Graduates of this program are encouraged to settle permanently off the reservation.

Despite the optimistic results stated in various BIA reports, this program has fallen far short of expectations, at least at AIS. Of those who initially enroll, over 40 per cent drop out before the five-year period is over. Of those who do graduate, at least 90 per cent return to the reservation by the end of a year. During my stay in Albuquerque, I contacted about fifteen graduates. It was obvious that they had painfully inadequate English language skills and only a fragmentary and distorted concept of Anglo living. They were patently unhappy with city life and soon returned to the reservation. Dissatisfaction with low-paying, unskilled jobs and a pervasive fear and distrust of most aspects of city living contributed to their return. I suspect that the brightest and most aggressive male graduates of this program joined the military service to facilitate a more thorough introduction to off-reservation life.

In 1956 the Public Health Service withdrew free medical care for Navajos at Bernalillo County Indian Hospital. The director of the Service told me in 1960 that the scope of free services made available was governed by the limits of personnel and budget for a given area. Apparently the Public Health Service could no longer afford to give free medical assistance to local Navajos. Strangely enough, however, it continued to extend free care to resident Pueblo Indians.

This withdrawal of aid caused some hardship among many of the poorer Navajos with large families. It also infuriated their more prosperous fellow tribesmen. The action had three interesting results: (1) the formation of a slight group consciousness among resident Navajos because they once more had a common and familiar enemy, the Federal Government; (2) closer contacts with Window Rock, since the Albuquerque Navajos began to appeal unsuccessfully to the Tribal Council for aid; (3) the formation of an Albuquerque Navajo Club which was a rather pathetic attempt to rectify this and other real or imagined injustices.

GENERAL CHARACTERISTICS OF THE CURRENT (1959-1961) NAVAJO POPULATION

During my residence in Albuquerque from July, 1959, through June, 1961, 275 adult (eighteen years and over) Navajos lived in town. There were never more than 180 to 200 Navajos in residence at a given time. This aggregate will be generally characterized as to migration pattern, cultural orientation, age, sex, marriage pattern, type of occupation, income, social grouping and voluntary organization, urban participation, language facility, deviant behavior, and daily behavior.

Migration Patterns

Original reservation and off-reservation locations of residents and their times of arrival in Albuquerque will be considered under this category. Special consideration is given to Canyoncito-Albuquerque relations since this small reservation is the largest single source of Navajo migrants.

ORIGINAL LOCATIONS OF ALBUQUERQUE NAVAJO MIGRANTS

It should be noted that residence in many cases was not necessarily "in" the community given in Table 3. Navajos refer to a community as "home" if it is the nearest mail drop or trading post to their family's camp or hogan.

It is evident that the majority of Albuquerque Navajos are from the eastern half of the reservation.

TABLE 3
RESERVATION AND OFF-RESERVATION ORIGINS OF NAVAJO MIGRANTS TO ALBUQUERQUE

Place of Origin	Number of Migrants	Place of Origin	Number of Migrants
Alamo	4	Manuelito	2
Albuquerque	4	Many Farms	1
Aneth	1	Many Lakes	1
Buffalo Springs	2	Mariano Lake	1
Canyoncito	30	Nageesi	3
Cabezon	1	Naschitti	1
Chambers	1	Nasklaa	1
Chandler	1	Newcomb	3
Chicago, Illinois	1	Prewitt	1
Chinle	6	Rattlesnake	4
Coolidge	3	Redrock	1
Cornfields	3	St. Michaels	7
Crownpoint	9	Sanders	1
Crystal	5	Sheepsprings	1
Deer Springs	1	Shiprock	8
Farmington	5	Teec Nos Pos	11
Flagstaff	3	Tees Toh	1
Fort Defiance	9	Toadlena	5
Fort Wingate	5	Tohatchi	16
Gallup	18	Torreon	5
Ganado	8	Tuba City	3
Greasewood	1	Twin Lakes	3
Holbrook	1	Unknown	62
Indian Wells	1	Warm Springs	1
Isleta	1	Wildcat Springs	2
Kayenta	1	Window Rock	2
Lukachukai	2		

As Hillery and Essene (1963: 303) point out, this may be partially due to the fact that this region is the most heavily populated area.

TIMES OF ARRIVAL IN ALBUQUERQUE

A few Navajos moved into Albuquerque from 1907 to 1946, but most of the city's Navajo population arrived during the post-war periods, 1946–50 and 1955-58 (Table 4).

Although it was impossible to obtain adequate data regarding those leaving the city for other urban areas or the reservation, it appears that the Albuquerque population is a stable one. By October, 1959, a roster of residents had been made. Throughout the duration of field work, various informants were asked to tell what they knew about those Navajos who had left the city. Within the twenty-two months of research, 19 families consisting of 38 adults, an unknown number of children, and eight single individuals, returned to the reservation. This is about 20 per cent of the Navajos in the city. One family and one single individual moved to another urban area. I have no data as to how these

TABLE 4
NUMBER OF NAVAJO MIGRANTS TO ALBUQUERQUE BY YEAR OF ARRIVAL, 1907-61

Year	Number	Year	Number	Year	Number
1907	1	1926	1	1945	1
1908	0	1927	0	1946	20
1909	0	1928	2	1947	20
1910	0	1929	0	1948	10
1911	0	1930	0	1949	19
1912	1	1931	0	1950	27
1913	0	1932	0	1951	5
1914	0	1933	0	1952	0
1915	0	1934	2	1953	1
1916	0	1935	2	1954	4
1917	0	1936	2	1955	11
1918	0	1937	1	1956	20
1919	0	1938	2	1957	25
1920	0	1939	1	1958	12
1921	0	1940	1	1959	6
1922	2	1941	0	1960	7
1923	0	1942	1	1961	4
1924	0	1943	1	Unknown	63
1925	1	1944	0		

figures compare to the out-migration of the non-Navajo resident population during this same period.

THE CANYONCITO NAVAJOS

R. J. Kurtz gathered data here over an eighteen-month field period. He states (1963: 186) that the agricultural economy of the reservation can support but a fraction of its population. Only 275 out of 624 enrolled Navajos reside permanently on the reservation. This may well be a higher proportion of enrolled off-reservation residents than exists on the large reservation. In a 1960 letter to me he summarized the reservation-urban residence pattern:

... there are three main categories of Canyoncito Navajo who are sometimes or usually in urban areas. (1) Those who are there most of the time and are occupied fairly regularly at supporting jobs; (2) there are those who are perennial in-and-outers who may work for a while at Alameda, then at Bluewater, then up at Colorado in fruit, or at Las Lunas in fruit, or down at Socorro in cotton, and then do a stint at silversmithing, and so on through the possibilities, maybe doing one of these things during a year, while working at nearby ranches for part of the year, and goofing off the rest — a whole series of permutations [are possible here]; and (3) those who are described by the Canyoncito people as being "on First Street" or "on skid row," a whole bunch of characters who have no visible means of support, but who manage to stay drunk day in and day out, until they are put in jail for thirty days, when they start it again. There are also some in-and-outers

in this category. I have never figured out how these people lived.

Most of the thirty Canyoncito people living in Albuquerque during my stay there fall within the first of these categories. Prudence, or perhaps sheer cowardliness, prevented me from learning much about those in the third category. Local law enforcement agencies could provide little data on Canyoncito drunks.

Cultural Orientation

Forty-two of the 275 Albuquerque Navajo residents are permanent-resident, 78 are Anglo-modified, and 58 are traditional. An additional 12 are not permanent-resident, but I do not know what subcategory they belong in. The cultural orientation of 85 people is unknown.

Age and Sex

The Albuquerque Navajo population is young; not more than thirteen individuals are over fifty. Most Navajos are between the ages of twenty and forty (Table 5). There are 140 men and 135 women.

TABLE 5
AGE DISTRIBUTION OF ALBUQUERQUE NAVAJOS, 1959-61

Age	Frequency
18-30	92
30-40	65
40-50	40
50-60	10
60-70	3
Unknown	65

Marriage and Family Patterns

There are 112 families. About 60 per cent of these Navajos were married before they came to Albuquerque. About 40 per cent of them came to the city as single individuals and then married. There are 29 single men and 53 single women. Navajos show a strong preference for Navajo spouses (Table 6).

The non-Navajo spouse marriages consist of: 11 Navajo men married to Anglo women; 3 Navajo women married to Anglo men; 17 Navajo men married to other-Indian women; 2 Navajo women married to other-Indian men; 5 Navajo men married to "Spanish" women; 4 Navajo women married to "Spanish" men; and 3 Navajo men married to women whose ethnic identity is unknown to me. Navajo men show a greater tendency to marry non-Navajo spouses than do Navajo women.

Most marriages were performed by a Justice of the Peace. This is probably due to the fact that

TABLE 6
ALBUQUERQUE NAVAJO MARRIAGE BY ETHNIC IDENTITY OF SPOUSE

Ethnic Identity of Spouse	Frequency
Navajo	67
Other-Indian	19
Anglo	14
"Spanish"	9
Unknown	3
Total	112

most Navajos have little interest in Christianity. A Navajo couple wary of Anglo customs may also find a Justice of the Peace easier to approach than a clergyman.

All families are neolocal in residence. The parents and other older kinsmen of the Navajo residents were either dead or living on the reservation. In no more than twelve cases did an unmarried sibling of one of the spouses live in the home on a temporary basis. Only four of the families had no children. The number of children per family ranged from one to seven, with a mode of three.

With the exception of a few of the Special Program graduates, single individuals lived alone.

Type of Occupation

A wide range of occupations are held, varying from dishwashing machine operator to mechanical engineer. Most jobs are in the semi-skilled and skilled categories (Table 7). The one occupation followed with greatest frequency is that of silversmith, with 32 individuals working at this trade. Most of these Navajos have a traditional orientation, but six can be classified as Anglo-modified. Silversmithing is a skill which can be learned in six months or a year, but it is an unpleasant occupation. Wages are low. Silversmithing frequently causes eye damage after four or five years. Most of these people have trouble with liquor and many claim to be bothered by witches (Hodge, 1967: 18–59).

The single employer hiring the largest number of Navajos (a total of 25) is the United Pueblo Agency (UPA) of the Bureau of Indian Affairs. Here, as throughout the Bureau, Indians are given preference in hiring over other ethnic classifications.

It is interesting to note that in the strictest

TABLE 7
OCCUPATIONS OF ALBUQUERQUE NAVAJOS BY FREQUENCY AND SEX, 1959-61

Occupation	Male	Female
Auto mechanic	3	0
AIS handymen	2	0
Baker	3	0
BIA teacher	5	3
Cabinet maker	2	0
Cafeteria worker	0	12
Carpenter	1	0
Civil engineer UPA	1	0
Clerk	4	2
Clerk UPA	0	1
Construction UPA	1	0
Construction worker	10	0
Dairy worker	1	0
Delivery man	1	0
Dishwasher	3	0
Electronics technician	6	0
Engineer	1	0
Filling station attendant	4	0
Housewife	0	42
Interpreter UPA	5	2
Janitor	1	0
Kirtland AFB (civilian worker)	2	0
Laborer	1	0
Part-time laborer	2	0
Leather worker	1	0
Linen room attendant, Presbyterian Hospital	0	11
Linotype operator	1	0
Machinist	2	0
Maid	0	2
Meter repair technician	1	0
Minister	1	0
Newspaperman	1	0
Nursery worker	6	0
Office manager	1	0
Office worker	3	0
Paint contractor	1	0
Painter-construction	2	0
Painter, UPA	2	0
Plumber	4	0
Powerhouse worker, UPA	2	0
Practical nurse	0	6
Prostitute	0	6
Registered nurse	0	1
Retired	1	0
Salesman	2	0
Secretary	0	2
Sheet metal worker	1	0
Silversmith	25	7
Social worker	2	0
Student nurse	1	0
University of New Mexico student (married, spouse in residence)	7	0
Traffic policeman	1	0
Typist	1	0
Unknown occupation	61	
Waitress AIS	0	1
Weaver	0	1
X-Ray technician	0	1

sense, there are no unemployed Navajos in Albuquerque, disregarding housewives and the Canyoncito transient drunks. The two "part-time" laborers do not hold regular jobs because of poor health. One is supported by his wife and the other by his brother-in-law.

Income

Incomes for 99 per cent of the Navajos are adequate in that they can provide food, clothing, and shelter for themselves in necessary quantities. However, the majority of residents live well above a marginal standard. A basic ecological factor would seem to account for this. Albuquerque is far enough away from the reservation that friends and relatives can not readily aid Albuquerque Navajos should they be willing and able to do so. Aid from tribal, local, state, and federal sources is nil. Hence, virtually any Navajo who lives in Albuquerque must be economically independent. Such a situation is not found in reservation border towns such as Farmington, Gallup, and Flagstaff where it is suspected that less economically self-reliant Navajos reside.

Almost all Anglo-modified and all permanent-resident Navajos refused to discuss their incomes and spending habits with me. I was told that this was "none of my business." For this reason, 1960 census data are relied upon. Annual incomes for Anglo-modified and permanent-resident Navajos ranged between $4,000 and $15,000. The traditionals did not show this reluctance to disclose income figures. Their annual incomes ranged between $1,200 and $3,000, enough to insure little more than urban survival.

Social Grouping

As will be discussed later, the 275 Albuquerque Navajos constitute an aggregate, not a group. With the exception of the small number of traditionally oriented individuals, some of whom are peyotists and/or who knew each other before coming to Albuquerque, a marked, continuous, and successful effort is made by Navajos to avoid other tribal members in the city. Various specious reasons are given for this, but essentially Navajos appear to avoid each other because they fear that such associations will be to their economic detriment. As one informant said, "Once you are nice to a Navajo and feed him, he will be around all the time and that's bad."

In some cases, this avoidance can reach surprising extremes. Brad Wheeler came to Albuquerque from Ramah in 1941. When I questioned him in 1960,

he told me that the last Navajo he had talked to was his brother who left town in 1943 to live in San Francisco. I interviewed him at a garage where he worked as an auto mechanic. My identification of him as a Navajo caused him considerable embarrassment since he had told his employer and fellow workers that he was "Spanish." He said that he kept away from other Navajos because he "wanted to live clean." Wheeler was married to an Anglo woman. He refused to give me his address. I learned of Wheeler from a local Zuni.

Such avoidance is partially reflected in the residence pattern and the attenuated forms of voluntary organizations. As was noted earlier, most Navajos tend to live in medium- to low-cost housing areas, but residence clustering does not exist. Currently there are no all-Navajo or even all-Indian neighborhoods (Fig. 3).

During the first half of my stay in Albuquerque, there were a few Navajos living closely together in the employees' housing unit at AIS. However, this unit was closed, and the occupants had to live elsewhere. When the families found other housing, they were scattered over the northwest section of town.

Voluntary organizations have a tenuous existence because of a lack of support and an absence of apparent common interests. Factionalism with roots in tribal government upheaval and local disputes also contribute to this situation. A "Navajo Club" had been formed a few months prior to the beginning of this study. The *Navajo Times* (Feb. 1960: 6) states that the purpose of the club is

to provide general information concerning current and proposed tribal regulations, the various projects being considered by the Tribe and provide a means whereby those Navajos living off the reservation may get together and get acquainted with one another.

During the period of my study the first two goals were stressed rather than the last. The meetings of the club did bring some of the local Navajo residents together, but very few got acquainted by this means. Those who did were of comparable socioeconomic status. There were never more than twenty-five to thirty members who paid the dues of $1.00 per year. Of this number, not more than six or seven people were willing to do any work.

Meetings were rambling and aimless. Traditional Navajos did not feel comfortable there because Navajo was seldom spoken. The permanent-resident and Anglo-modified members resented translating the proceedings into Navajo "because it makes the damn meeting last too long." Without translation, the meetings lasted between three and four hours. Those attending were highly aloof toward each other. Families arrived separately, sat together, and then left immediately after light refreshments were served. As one informant put it, "they just sit there like stumps. You'd think that they were mad at or scared of each other." The only charitable project that the club undertook was to collect small amounts of food and clothing to give to the "poorer Navajos" in town during the Christmas season. During the two holiday periods that I lived in Albuquerque, the club asked me to select the families to receive these gifts and then to distribute them. I was also asked to make a brief report regarding this distribution early the following month. No other interest was shown in the recipients.

The club's president put forth a great deal of effort, but he seemed to be using his office as a springboard to a job with the Tribe on the reservation. In 1947, he had had a job with the Tribe, but quit because the "work was too hard and the pay was too low." Six months before I left, he did get a job as a BIA school teacher near the reservation. About a year after that, he was elected to a state school board office, defeating an Anglo incumbent.

Currently (1965), the club is still in existence, but I know little of its nature or activities. It does have a booth in the "Indian Village" at the annual State Fair.

The Albuquerque Navajo peyote situation can be outlined briefly. Approximately 25 out of the 275 resident Navajos are active members in the Native American Church (NAC). These people have a traditional or Anglo-modified orientation. They are poorly educated, in financial trouble, have English language difficulties, and are constantly worried about being publicly recognized as peyotists.

George Two Bears, a Crow who is president of the NAC, has characterized them as "frightened cattle." It is my impression that there is little or no contact between Two Bears, who is living in Albuquerque, and these 25 individuals. To them he remains a rather nebulous and remote figure. They follow such occupations as silversmithing, construction, and agricultural work. Both husband and wife, and quite often the family children, are Church members. I suspect that all of them do not rely solely on peyote for the treatment of illness. Some of them are "reformed" alcoholics who have turned to peyote to stop drinking. I know of two Navajo residents who were users, but have given it up. Most

Church meetings are held on Saturday night from sundown to sunup at Canyoncito. Some peyotists attend services at their home reservation communities when they visit there. The meetings at Canyoncito are held "at least every two weeks and not more than three times a month." Those attending, besides the Albuquerque Navajos, are from Gallup, Alamo, Ramah, "and a lot of other people that we don't know." One prominent Church member living in Albuquerque holds services at his house on Easter — "people come from as far away as Holbrook; we have it at my house because there is no place else."

The use of peyote seemed to vary independently with desirable or undesirable character traits possessed. Some users were liked and respected by all those who knew them, while others were not.

Peyote equipment and the buttons themselves come from various sources. A Potawatomi from Oklahoma has a small shop in Old Town and sells fans, rattles, boxes, ladders, and staffs which he obtains from Oklahoma. These are quite expensive; a moderately good fan costs $65, and a ladder sells for $40. Many local peyotists buy equipment there on time, and this man always has a considerable stock on lay-away. He also sells buttons for $16 per thousand, which he gets near Laredo, Texas, at $10 per thousand. With the exception of fans, some users make their own equipment. Some of it is given to them by friends and relatives on the reservation. A few of the Navajos reputedly go to southwest Texas themselves to harvest peyote.

The peyotists visit each other, both as single individuals and as families. Some material aid is exchanged, but because of their low incomes this is never very much. These people, like others with traditional orientations, are suspicious and resentful toward permanent-resident Navajos and some Anglo-modified tribesmen because they feel that somehow they have advanced themselves materially at their expense. A frequently heard expression is "a peyote man is worth ten Navajos with college degrees."

There was an all-Navajo Pentecostal church located in the South Valley. Of the total Navajo population in Albuquerque of 275, not more than ten adults took any part in the church's activities. These had known each other before coming to the city either through ties of friendship or kinship. According to the church staff and those of the congregation who were questioned, at least 75 per cent of the Navajo congregation lived at Canyoncito. The rest lived at Alamo and in the Checkerboard area, particularly the Smith Lake Region. I have commented on the activities of this organization elsewhere (Hodge, 1964: 73–93).

At the beginning of this study most Albuquerque Navajos seemed to be surprisingly ignorant regarding the number and locations of tribal members in town. Most of those whom I contacted in the first months of work seriously doubted if there could be more than forty or fifty other Navajo residents, and little curiosity was shown as to learning more about their fellow tribesmen. This ignorance also extended to the Tribal Council headquarters at Window Rock, Arizona, and the local Bureau of Indian Affairs Office.

Urban Participation

Albuquerque Navajos do not appear to be overly fond of joining Anglo urban organizations. About 25 per cent of the veterans belonged to the American Legion or the Veterans of Foreign Wars but were not active. When necessary, the skilled workers belonged to appropriate trade unions. Church affiliation was correspondingly low. Thirty-three residents were at least nominal Catholics, about twelve belonged to the Christian Reformed Church, and five claimed to be Baptists.

Language Facility

Ninety-five per cent of the Navajos speak fair to excellent English. Five per cent speak Navajo only. It is suspected that at least 40 per cent of the residents had difficulty speaking effective Navajo. I was cautioned by one of my Navajo interpreters not to try to speak to permanent residents in Navajo, "because they'll think that you think they are stupid and don't know much English."

Daily Urban Behavior

Albuquerque Navajos go about their daily routine of urban living in much the same way as do the other residents of the city. Since all income must be provided by wage labor, many of their activities are regulated by the demands of steady employment. Most men work from 9:00 a.m. to 5:00 p.m. except for those who do shift work. The majority of women are housewives with children to care for. All children who are old enough attend public schools. There are no more than twelve Navajos over eighteen years of age who were born and reared in Albuquerque. Half of these were in the service when I

lived there. Two had died, one attended the university, and three worked at clerical jobs.

The Albuquerque Navajos wear the same sort of clothing that Anglos do, furnish their houses in as modern a fashion as their incomes permit, enjoy such urban leisure time activities as TV, movies, moderate drinking in local taverns, and card games. With two exceptions, the traditionals owned TV sets. Their older children spoke and understood English, and the parents felt that television was one means for them to learn English themselves. The traditionals were also fascinated by programs devoted to sports events and complex technological developments, such as rockets, satellites, and nuclear weapons. All but four families owned cars. Thirty per cent of the families had two cars. Most single people did not have automobiles and had to depend upon inadequate public transportation. More Navajos than Anglos attended the annual Gallup Intertribal Ceremonial and the Tribal Fair at Window Rock.

I found little discrimination against Navajos in Albuquerque. One Navajo single woman said that she had difficulty finding housing because of her background. Her brother said that he lost a job because his employer didn't like the way he looked. Another man stated that those of his tribe had to work harder to achieve the same rewards others got for less labor. However, most traditional and Anglo-modified Navajos seemed to have pronounced feelings of superiority regarding other ethnic groups. Their attitudes paralleled closely those described by Kluckhohn and Leighton (1946: 114–20) for the reservation dwellers. An expression frequently heard was, "Hell, I'm no damn Indian — I'm a Navajo!" Permanent-resident Navajos seemed to exhibit the same feelings toward other ethnic groups that local Anglos do.

Permanent-resident Navajos and at least half the Anglo-modified Navajos had only non-Navajo "friends" in the city. Most of these were Anglos. A "friend" is defined as a desirable person to spend leisure time with, attending sports events, visiting with each other in the house or yard, and relying upon each other for emotional or financial assistance in time of emergency. Most friends were neighbors or co-workers.

Many of the Anglo-modified Navajos had no friends and had lived virtually isolated since arriving in town and were prepared to continue to do so. Nor had they any reservation contacts to speak of.

As was discussed above, the traditionals did not

associate with permanent-resident and Anglo-modified Navajos because of a language barrier and financial handicaps. They also did not associate with other ethnic groups.

Traditional Navajo activities, for the most part, were absent. I know of one silversmith and his wife who when drunk danced "squaw dance" style all night in their living room, accompanying themselves by beating a Paiute drum. Three traditional women had vertical looms which they often used. One woman "jerked" meat. However, no sings were held while I was there, and no one lived in a hogan.

There was some interest shown in clan affiliation and exogamy. All Navajos felt that they and their children should not marry people from their own clan. One Navajo who had an Anglo wife and an adopted son said that his boy belonged to his maternal grandmother's clan. *All* Navajos contacted knew what clan they were in.

For permanent-resident Navajos, the important reservation units of social organization were the neolocal family and local community. For Anglo-modified and traditional Albuquerque Navajos the "local clan element" and local community were the significant units.

D. F. Aberle (1961: 108) discusses the local clan element:

This unit consists of the members of a given clan residing in a given area, plus some of the close relatives of these members living in nearby areas. It is loosely organized and constitutes the unilineal unit of collective responsibility and joint action. It is, of course, exogamic. In the literature we read of one "clan" proceeding against another, or of the members of a "clan" cooperating to give a ceremony. The dispersion and size of most clans make it impossible to believe that the clan in fact organized in any such way. It is necessary to assume that some local section of a clan took action, and this section I have termed a local clan element.

Elsewhere (p. 113), he notes:

the informant, speaking from the perspective of his own and neighboring communities, can perfectly well *say,* "If I am ill, *my clan* will help with the ceremony," and mean *the clan members he knows.*

It is significant that in Albuquerque I was able to find only two Navajos who belonged to the *same* local clan element. A relationship of fragmentary and reluctant mutual assistance prevailed. Many of them belonged to the same clans — Bitter Water, Standing House, Red Streak, and others — but this relationship apparently was too vague to foster expectations of mutual aid. When returning to the reservation, the traditionals interacted closely with their immediate families and other members of their local clan element. However, for previously mentioned reasons, the Anglo-modified Navajos regarded those of their local clan element largely as a source of annoyance.

Deviant Behavior

It is important to note that with a very few glaring exceptions, the Albuquerque Navajos seemed to be orderly and law-abiding. Those who did come to the attention of the police were arrested for drunken and disorderly conduct and minor offenses stemming from such behavior.

Six of the women were prostitutes. Their existence was a dreary cycle of plying their trade, living in cheap rooming houses and drinking on Skid Row with frequent intervals of "rest" spent in the local jail for drunken and disorderly conduct. Their time in jail was devoted to passive sullenness which was often interrupted by visits to the PHS clinic for the treatment of venereal disease.

There was one Navajo transvestite from Canyoncito living in town who worked as a "counter man" in a cheap restaurant near Skid Row. To my knowledge, he lived quietly in Albuquerque, but those from Canyoncito hated and feared him for allegedly having malevolent supernatural power.

There was some evidence that many Anglo-modified Navajos and all traditionals felt themselves to be potentially or actually threatened by witchcraft. These witches were not in town but on the reservation. One Anglo-modified Navajo, a silversmith, told me that he had been the victim of a witch's power while living in town. As he put it, "all at once I knew that I was goin' to die because somebody back on the reservation hates me." He promptly hired a "curer" at Jemez Pueblo to discover the identity of the witch and remove its influence. Another Navajo resident was attacked by a witch while visiting Canyoncito.

SUMMARY AND CONCLUSIONS

The purpose of these two chapters has been to provide a setting for viewing the Albuquerque Navajo data. The general sociocultural and temporal dimensions of the setting have been emphasized to provide a necessary perspective for the study of the Albuquerque Navajos.

Albuquerque and the reservation with its traditional and transitional communities are conceived as complementary parts of the same system. The forces which move Navajos from one part of the system to another have been discussed and the movements of specific Navajos have been used to illustrate these forces in operation.

Navajos have lived in Albuquerque for at least 75 years. It is suggested that their mode of occupa- tion has been uniform throughout this time. A few Navajos were forced to leave the reservation and came to Albuquerque to make a living. Their location in the city and general style of life depends largely upon their financial status. Most Navajos are able to procure the necessities of life in an urban environ- ment, but they prefer the reservation to the city. Most eventually return to the reservation to live.

5. THE PRODUCTS OF THE URBAN-RESERVATION SYSTEM

IT IS EVIDENT that for the Albuquerque Navajos the reservation and the city form parts of the same whole or system and that each Indian (excepting the permanent residents) occupies a sometimes stable, sometimes shifting place in it. The central purpose of this chapter will be the examination of the structure and operation of the urban-reservation system. Analysis will concentrate on the kinds of forces at work, the manner of their operation, and their possible effects.

After the mechanics of the system have been outlined, sixteen individuals representative of the three established cultural orientation categories (permanent-resident, traditional, and Anglo-modified) will be compared in an attempt to discover if certain factors are commonly associated with individuals in any one category. Such common factors as are found might prove or disprove, at least partially, the central and ancillary hypotheses posed by this study.

As a final step, extensive data on one individual from each of the three cultural orientation categories will be presented. This specific data will give substance to many aspects of urban and reservation migration and residence which heretofore have been referred to only in a general or abstract fashion.

THE MECHANICS OF THE SYSTEM

At this point the structure and operation of the urban-reservation system must be considered in

TABLE 8

PUSH AND PULL FORCES IN URBAN-RESERVATION SYSTEM THAT INFLUENCE THE INDIVIDUAL NAVAJO

Forces That Pull Individuals	Forces That Push Individuals
Away from urban orbit toward reservation orbit	**Toward urban orbit from reservation orbit**
1. Congenial family ties	1. Poverty
2. More relaxed atmosphere	2. Friction with relatives
3. Chance to use urban-acquired skills to best advantage	3. BIA schooling influences
4. Appearance of traditional niche unavailable before	4. Non-Navajo spouse
5. Appearance of non-traditional niche unavailable before	5. (Extreme) physical handicap
6. Inability to make a living in the city regarded as certain	6. Military service
7. Language barriers	
8. Unfulfilled obligations to reservation kinsmen	
Away from reservation orbit toward urban orbit	**Toward reservation orbit from urban orbit**
1. Opportunity for job	1. Unsatisfactory job aspirations
2. Escape from unsatisfactory reservation life	2. Lack of satisfying inter-personal urban relations
3. Higher standard of material living	3. General dissatisfaction with urban way of life
4. Medical care	4. Navajo spouse
5. Urban life preferable to or for children	
6. Inability to make a living on the reservation regarded as certain	
7. Language barriers	

detail, with emphasis placed on those forces operating within this environment which influence residence. The system has been said to consist of two orbits; a reservation orbit and an urban orbit. These orbits, as they relate to the Albuquerque Navajos, have been described in Chapter 2. With few exceptions, Navajos simultaneously experience push and pull forces toward and away from the urban orbit and toward and away from the reservation orbit (Table 8).

A number of points should be kept in mind when interpreting Table 8: (a) Push-pull forces account for movement or its absence within the system, working either alone or in combination; (b) This *formulation* is over-simplified, since other orbits such as Pueblo, rural "Spanish," planned seasonal movement between the reservation, and specific non-urban employment (for example, railroad work, harvesting, and seasonal crops) do exist; (c) The Navajos here termed permanent-resident by definition constitute a stable part of the urban orbit and are not subject to the various forces, while those termed non-permanent — resident most certainly are; (d) The reservation orbit consists of two types of reservation communities, traditional and transitional, which have been discussed above; and (e) The specific examples of the push and pull forces have been taken from the life histories, supplementary field notes, and other materials described in the preceding chapter.

The explanatory power of this scheme is tentative or heuristic. It is not the intent of this study to derive postulates to account for the residence patterns of all Albuquerque Navajos. All the specific pushes and pulls do not necessarily operate for every given Navajo. It may well be that some factors are more important than others in determining type of residence and hence should be weighted. However, such a task is beyond the scope of this study and is left to more quantitative modes of analysis in the future.

ISOLATION OF COMMON FACTORS

Sixteen Navajos were selected for intensive study on the basis of their willingness to cooperate. Intuitively, these sixteen seem to represent the range of Navajo types in Albuquerque. Further, they seem to be quite similar to ninety-two additional Navajo residents with whom I was moderately acquainted.

Hence, the limits of extrapolation are not confined to the sixteen individuals. Of the sixteen studied, three were permanent-resident, three wanted to return to a traditional reservation life, and ten hoped to live in the transitional reservation communities.

To facilitate analysis, the comparative data from the schedule and supplementary notes will be reduced to twelve factors. As previously noted, the common characteristics isolated are of immediate relevance in testing the hypotheses advanced at the beginning of this study.

Permanent-resident Navajos

Bruce Jesson, John Powell, and **Pat James.**

1. Name: all lack a Navajo name.
2. Age: no patterning is shown in age. Jesson is 45; Powell, 27; James, 28.
3. Ethnic identity: all are full-blooded.
4. Language: their Navajo-speaking ability is fair to non-existent.
5. Reservation background: all had a relatively open reservation background and were subjected to a number of non-Navajo influences. For various reasons all had parents who did not serve as models for a traditional Navajo life and/or were subjected to traditional influences only for a short time.

Jesson's father was "divorced" by his mother and Jesson "never saw him again." Since his mother spent most of her time in various BIA hospitals thereafter, Jesson lived for two to three years with his highly traditional maternal grandparents, but "didn't like this." Powell's father was an off-reservation miner much of his life. James' parents led non-Navajo lives on the reservation and followed western occupations.

All were subjected to non-Navajo influences at an early age through school (Jesson at age nine, Powell and James at age six). All had fewer than three siblings and were the oldest child in their respective families. All three were obliged to leave the reservation and left their reservation homes as children.

They state that their contacts with relatives and friends on the reservation are generally of a pleasant and satisfying nature. They agree that the reservation may be a good place for some Navajos to live, but not for them.

6. Military service: James has had military service; Jesson and Powell were 4-F.
7. Marital factors: all are married to non-Navajos; James to a forty-five-year-old Anglo woman; Powell to a Pueblo; Jesson to a Jicarilla. All were married by a Justice of the Peace. Their wives have all indicated in one way or another that they would not enjoy a reservation existence.
8. Education: all three have had at least a high school education and have a good to excellent command of English. They have a good to excellent knowledge of the Anglo world and enjoy their urban existences.
9. Subsistence: all have a good to excellent level of subsistence due to the type of employment held. They appear to be satisfied with and/or to enjoy their jobs. Jesson is a machine operator, Powell a journeyman electrician, and James a well-supported student. Their spouses work at well-paying full- or part-time jobs. Finances appear to be well managed by Anglo standards. Little or no aid is given relatives on the reservation. Dwellings and furnishings range from adequate to excellent. All appear to be thoroughly imbued with the idea that hard work, careful planning, and thrift will lead to "success and security."
10. Religious orientation: there is virtually no knowledge of, or reverence for, traditional ceremonial practice. Most other aspects of traditional Navajo culture are either ignored or openly scorned. The idea of witchcraft constitutes only a source of amusement. Orthodox forms of Christianity are either ignored or taken lightly. Pentecostal Christianity and peyote are regarded as "silly."
11. Social orbit: reservation visits occur no more often than once every three to four years and are never more than a few hours duration. Letters and/or telephone calls are exchanged not more often than twice a year. (James hasn't been to his home for nine years.) With very rare exceptions urban Navajo contacts are carefully and deliberately avoided. The bulk of casual social friends are job associates and to a lesser extent neighbors, but "visits" or parties do not occur more than once a week.

Recreation consists of taking advantage of the facilities which any urban center can offer such as movies, bowling, and spectator sports. A considerable amount of time is spent watch-ing TV at home. Trips are taken with the family on holidays.

12. Idiosyncratic factors: Powell and James appear to be well adjusted, average middle class citizens. Jesson has an obsessive concern with his health which seems to amount to hypochondria.

Traditional Navajos

Joe Sandoval, Jeff Morrison, and **Herman Sanchez.**
1. Name: all have Navajo names.
2. Age: all are over thirty. This means that at least for the first few years of their lives the reservation had not been subjected to the pervasive changes which stock reduction, World War II, the industrialization of the Southwest, extensive off-reservation employment, increased BIA services, and other forces stimulated. (This generalization applies essentially to all non-permanent — resident Navajos.)
3. Ethnic identity: Morrison and Sanchez are full blooded. Joe Sandoval is not.
4. Language: all speak good Navajo.
5. Reservation background: all had a closed reservation background and were subjected to little or no direct non-Navajo influences. Their parents are all traditionally oriented; none had any non-Navajo contacts as children that appear to have been highly influential in their lives. What contact they did have seems to have been neutrally or negatively tinged. All have at least six siblings.

All were obliged to leave the reservation. Sandoval and Sanchez left for health reasons; Morrison moved because of extreme family poverty and because he wanted a public school education for his children. All left the reservation as adults.

All state that their contacts with relatives and friends on the reservation were generally of a pleasant and satisfying nature. They regard the reservation as a good place to live and hope to live with or near kinsmen should they return.
6. Military service: none has had military service.
7. Marital factors: Sandoval and Morrison were married "the Navajo way." Sanchez is single. Sandoval is divorced. Sandoval and Morrison have three children born on the reservation by non-English speaking Navajo women whose reservation backgrounds and off-reservation experiences resemble their own.
8. Education: all have little or no formal educa-

tion, speak only Navajo with any facility, and have the barest knowledge of and association with the non-Navajo world. They regard the latter as a difficult and sometimes dangerous place to live.

9. Subsistence: all have a marginal level of subsistence because they can perform only unskilled labor and have extremely low incomes. Little interest or satisfaction is shown in their work. Their perilous financial situation is aggravated by the fact that they show a gross inability to manage their money effectively — at least, by "good" Anglo standards. For example, they aid friends and relatives with money, personal possessions, and labor to their own detriment; they purchase expensive western clothing and Navajo jewelry which they cannot afford; and Sandoval and Morrison have bought impractical second-hand cars. Dwellings and furnishings are of the barest and cheapest variety.

All are aware that their wages, jobs, and style of living are considerably below that of many Anglos and other Navajos, but little or no anxiety, embarrassment, or resentment is shown over this fact. Inadequate financial resources and all that this lack implies are borne stoically, and all state that as soon as traditional reservation residence can be resumed, life will become much more satisfactory.

10. Religious orientation: all have a great deal of reverence for, and some knowledge of, traditional ceremonial practice. If it were necessary and possible, such ceremonial practice would be utilized. Most other aspects of Navajo culture are revered. All seriously believe in witchcraft, and other means of relating to the supernatural have been or are being relied upon. Morrison is an active, dedicated peyotist and has some interest in Christianity. Sandoval and Sanchez have used peyote but now rely upon a rather aberrant form of Pentecostal Christianity.

11. Social orbit: all return to the reservation for visits with relatives and friends as frequently as possible. Visits may last several days or even weeks. Because of the distance from the reservation, transportation difficulties, and local job demands, this seldom occurs more than every four months. Within Albuquerque, casual visits with Anglos are unknown. Visiting is done with Navajos of similar orientation at least once a week. This visiting is done by whole families,

not single individuals. Those Navajos labeled here as Anglo-modified and permanent-resident are avoided because of the direct and indirect rebuffs which the traditional individuals have received from them.

Recreation consists of watching TV, sports events, and taking occasional hunting trips. Sandoval and Sanchez regard church activities as recreation.

12. Idiosyncratic factors: all show a pronounced concern over personal health. Professional medical aid and patent medicines are used whenever possible. As implied earlier, these traditional non-permanent — resident Navajos have little or no understanding and appreciation of urban western life. A traditional existence on the reservation is regarded as the most desirable way of life, but none of them can find a currently available niche on the reservation.

With the exception of anxiety over health and the partially related fear of witches, the three Navajos in this category seem to possess even temperaments and to meet life generally in an easy, relaxed fashion.

Anglo-modified Navajos

Joseph Barnes, Walter Higgins, Woody Carlson, Henry Chavez, Art Davis, Jack Fred, Nils Anderson, Hoot Prince, Marshall Tome, and Roger Ball.

1. Name: four individuals have a Navajo name (Higgins, Chavez, Fred, and Anderson); four do not (Carlson, Davis, Ball, and Tome). For two (Barnes and Prince), this fact is unknown.

2. Age: age ranges from 27 to 65. The majority fall between 27 and 45. Hence, at least the immediate families of all these people experienced reservation life as it was prior to stock reduction, World War II, and all the changes these two events brought with them.

3. Ethnic identity: with two exceptions, all are full blooded. Chavez had a Mescalero Apache mother; Fred had an Anglo grandfather.

4. Language: command of the Navajo language is poor to excellent.

5. Reservation background: all had a closed reservation background until they began to attend BIA school on the reservation when they were no older than twelve. Until this time they were subjected to little or no non-Navajo contacts. Those contacts that they did have were either neutrally or positively tinged. All had tradi-

tionally oriented parents and more than three siblings. All occupied the position of a younger and subordinate (less favored) child in the family.

The ten state that their contacts with relatives and friends on the reservation are frequently unpleasant and unsatisfying. All agree that the reservation is a good place to live provided certain improvements in living conditions are made. None of them necessarily want to live with or near kinsmen.

6. Military service: with the exception of Joseph Barnes, who is 4-F, all have had military service.

7. Marital factors: all are married. Six out of the ten have non-Navajo spouses. A much greater variety in background for spouses is shown than is the case with the traditional Navajos. All wives are highly ambivalent about living on the reservation.

Eight of the ten were married by a Justice of the Peace, and two were married by a church. None were married with a traditional ceremony. The number of children range from none to nine. Most have three. All children have been born and reared off the reservation.

8. Education: with three exceptions (Chavez, Anderson, and Ball), all have a high school diploma. Two, Higgins and Tome, have B.S. degrees. Ball has no more than a sixth grade education. Command of English ranges from fair to excellent. All have a good to excellent knowledge of the non-Navajo world and are able to make an adequate adjustment to it but find the pace, impersonality, and formality of urban living compared to reservation living to be quite irksome at times.

9. Subsistence: all have a fair to excellent level of subsistence because of the type of job held. All show a dissatisfaction with current employment, either stating a specific preference for another job and/or claiming that the present job is "dull," "underpaid," "insecure," or otherwise unsatisfactory. Four of the spouses work at full- or part-time jobs. Eight out of the ten own their own homes, one owns an elaborate trailer, and one rents a house. Dwellings and furnishings range from adequate to excellent. All own at least one car or pick-up; six own two vehicles.

Money is carefully managed, and a certain pride is shown in savings. Specific inquiries regarding salary, savings, and finances, however, are resented. Some form of aid is grudgingly given to immediate relatives on the reservation, and all ten freely state that they are often taken advantage of by relatives.

All seem to be dissatisfied with their material level of achievement. Their lack of "success," and dissatisfaction with their wages, type of jobs, style of living, and other aspects of their lives is a source of embarrassment and anxiety to them, at least this is so when they are talking with me.

10. Religious orientation: knowledge of and reverence for traditional ceremonial practice ranges from gross ignorance and skepticism to pervasive reverence and considerable knowledge. Fred and Carlson fall into the former category, while the remainder approach the latter. All express an apparently genuine regret about not knowing more about "the old ways." Fred and Carlson dismiss witches as "crazy ideas." The rest seem to accept witchcraft as a reality, and a few (Chavez, Tome, Ball, Anderson, and Higgins) regard it as a potential or actual threat. Only Anderson, Ball, and Tome have an active interest in orthodox Christianity, but it is regarded as merely another means of relating to the supernatural in addition to traditional practices. Chavez is an ardent Pentecostal.

11. Social orbit: reservation visits vary from once a year to every six weeks. Most people in this category visit the reservation two to three times a year in the summer or fall when traveling is easiest. Visits usually last for a weekend. Letters and/or telephone calls are exchanged at least once a month. Some (Higgins, Anderson, Ball, and Tome) express regret that contact with reservation relatives is not more frequent. The rest feel that their contacts are adequate. Social contacts with other Navajos in Albuquerque are avoided because "they will take advantage of you." Higgins, as president of the Navajo Club, has the greatest range of contacts, but these are not social. Tome, as my interpreter, had many "professional" contacts.

For the men, social contacts consist of job associates and former school friends. Their spouses share some of these relationships and "drink coffee" with other housewives living nearby. The frequency of such contacts averages twice a month. All ten complain of a lack of time for social contacts that is probably imaginary. Since such contacts usually involve money as well as time, they are probably deliberately held to this level. Joseph Barnes, Ball, and Prince are virtual recluses.

Available data suggest that a considerable amount of time is spent by almost all of these Navajos enjoying various spectator sports in season either alone or accompanied by immediate family members. With the exception of Chavez, a minimum of six hours a week is spent watching sporting events on TV. Chavez believes that TV will incite one to "evil and sin." All of Chavez's free time is spent "preaching the Gospel" to local Indians and Navajos at Canyoncito and Alamo.

12. Idiosyncratic factors: Walter Higgins has serious domestic problems and "a drinking problem." Chavez has such a Calvinistic approach to life that others have difficulty getting along with him. Ball is a moody extrovert who has stormy relations with everyone. Prince's behavior is highly egocentric and unpredictable. All those in this category are subject to surprising (at least in comparison with those in the other two categories) fluctuations of temperament, and it was impossible for me to isolate objective reasons for their sudden changes of mood. They have all had unpleasant experiences by virtue of the fact that they are urban residents. Tome and Higgins, two brothers, have returned to the reservation and live in separate transitional communities.

The implications of this material as regards the hypotheses of this study are positive. All common factors isolated for each of the three categories confirm the general descriptions of each type of Navajo presented earlier.

THREE ALBUQUERQUE NAVAJOS

In an effort to give depth to this study, three individual Navajos will be given extensive consideration: John Powell, permanent-resident; Joseph Sandoval, traditional; and Joseph Barnes, Anglo-modified. Powell, Sandoval, and Barnes were selected because they seem to represent their categories clearly. I also have relatively comprehensive data regarding them.

A condensed form of the life histories of these three Navajos is presented together with data taken from supplementary observations. Their current patterns of urban living are described. Emphasis is placed upon data concerning their movements between the reservation and Albuquerque and the factors associated with such residence changes. Where clarity and brevity of expression require it, direct quotes are used. There are situations where the data can and should speak for themselves. In a few instances, material relating to other Navajos in the same category are used to supplement the narration.

The order of the presentation of the case studies generally follows that of the field schedule. However, data presented in the previous section are not repeated here.

John Powell

Powell was a relaxed and confident individual. He was also a congenial informant and, with one exception, was willing to discuss all aspects of his life with me. He lived at Isleta Pueblo because he had married an Isleta woman. He seemed to have no interest in the traditional aspects of pueblo life. However, he was very reluctant to discuss his place in the pueblo and the activities of his affinal relatives there.

Powell was born in 1933 at Rattlesnake. His parents had no formal education, but his father could speak enough English to work effectively at various menial jobs. The effects of the stock reduction program reached the Powell family about 1937 when they were forced to give up most of their small livestock holdings. All their horses had to be sold and "there were only a few sheep left, just enough to fill one corral." The family had a small farm which could have been irrigated, but they had no implements for cultivation. Their few remaining sheep were moved to Powell's father's mother's herd, and his father went to work for the BIA on a nearby experimental farm.

Shortly after that, his father took some sort of job near Fort Wingate. During these preschool years Powell led a relatively pleasant life and spent most of his time playing with his younger brother and a cousin. His only other companions were his parents and his grandmother. Since his family had no livestock nearby, he had no herding responsibilities.

At age six he was sent to the Methodist Mission School at Farmington, which at that time probably offered the best academic training in the area. Discipline was harsh, but did not approach the excesses of the Albuquerque Indian School in the 1887 to 1929 period. His brother was soon enrolled there.

Powell enjoyed the studying but resented the discipline. When his brother was being whipped for some offense, he attempted to "clobber" the disciplinarian. As a result, both boys were beaten. Powell also "had all the Christian religion pounded out of me."

When he was ten, the family moved to Rico, Colorado, because his father had gotten a job in the mine there. He adjusted well to the elementary school and was delighted with sports such as baseball and basketball. He and his brother were immediately accepted by the white school children and their parents and were included in most of the appropriate community activities. However, his parents were isolated in Rico because of their lack of education and English language skills.

During this period Powell's family went back to Rattlesnake three or four times in the summer to visit their relatives and take part in the squaw dances. The parents enjoyed these dances, but Powell didn't "because I just couldn't sing right." He had a sing about this time for severe headaches which was effective. "A hand trembler told my mother that when she was pregnant with me my father had seen some human bones, and this had caused it all." The entire procedure was a source of great amusement to Powell.

The years passed pleasantly for Powell, and he completed the eight available years of schooling in Rico. His family decided to send him to AIS for high school training because he wanted to go there. While at the Intertribal Ceremonial in Gallup one year he had seen some Navajo boys wearing the school's athletic letter sweaters, and he wanted to acquire one for himself.

In 1947, at age fourteen, he came to Albuquerque. The city seemed large and somewhat forbidding at first, but by the end of his freshman year, he had come to enjoy the urban environment. He did well in athletics and maintained a "B" average in his classroom work. Powell also met Ann, whom he would marry four years later. The summer of his freshman year he returned to Rico, but was soon "very lonesome" for Albuquerque.

During his sophomore year his father became seriously ill and had to quit mine work. His parents then worked in the vegetable harvests in southern Arizona. His father soon died. Powell wanted to leave school to help his mother but she insisted that he continue his education. His father had also wanted him to graduate from high school.

One of the male teachers took a special interest in Powell, and he thought about going to college to study mining engineering. Because of his precarious financial position, he later realized that he would never have the means to go to college, so he decided to become an electrician because he enjoyed the training that AIS offered in this area. During the summers until his graduation he worked at skilled jobs in construction at Shiprock and in Colorado and Utah. When he graduated, he was accepted by the electricians' union to enter an apprentice program, but it was about six months before he could begin work. He worked at various odd jobs in Albuquerque and Phoenix and then was hired on a permanent basis by Western Electric as an assembler and installer of complex equipment for telephone switchboard centers.

About this time, he narrowly escaped being jailed for drunken and disorderly conduct at a dance at the Indian School. A note in his school record dated October 2, 1951, reads as follows:

Letter from C. W. Franklin to Mr. Fred Williams, Principal: Please write a letter to John in no uncertain terms that we can do without his presence hereafter on the campus as he came out to the school last Saturday night in an intoxicated condition and engaged in a fight with a person by the name of Tony from Isleta. After the fight I immediately collared him and told Mr. Dave Coleman to take the advisor's car and get him off campus immediately or take him to jail. Dave reported he jumped out of the window of the car and made a get-away. I would have had the Police come out and pick him up but I had to get rid of him write (sic) away as he was creating a disturbance.

Powell tried to enlist in the Navy and the Air Force but was rejected because of a football injury. When he was hired by Western Electric, he married Ann Najarano of Isleta. When I contacted him, he had worked for this employer for eight years and hoped to continue to do so until he retired. He seemed to derive a great deal of satisfaction from his job:

It's really interesting. It's everything that we do. . . . No routine, not like the maintenance of a telephone office. . . . We start with a brand new telephone office, there's nothing in the telephone office to begin with except the building and we install superstructure made of iron and we solder and put them together from drawings. Then we run our cables and then we connect them up to the equipment according to drawings. Then we test them to see if it works. Then when we find that it does work we turn it over to the telephone company. And it's theirs from there. . . . Like I say there's some routine all right, like putting it together but after you get in the testing stage it's really interesting, you get all lost in there. Have quite a time . . . we work anything that's in communication. . . . And that's to me just interesting.

In 1962 Isleta had a population of about 1,900. Powell and his family lived in a small area on the east side of the Rio Grande. Parsons (1932: 208) describes this section:

On the eastern side there is a settlement of about six houses, the people of which are referred to as . . . earth yellow people. . . . White Village people, who are said to be "mean people," also to speak a little differently, dialectically, from the townspeople proper.

When I interviewed Powell in 1960, there was a single rectangular structure here. His wife's parents lived in one-half of this. The residences had separate entrances and were separated inside by a thick adobe wall. Their home was given to them by his wife's father's brother. Powell cooperated fully with the pueblo authorities and with his wife's parents. His son and two daughters spoke English and Tiwa but not Navajo. His wife and children were active in the appropriate societies — possibly the Corn Groups — and participated in public dancing when asked. Powell commented nervously, "I don't agree with them or disagree with them or anything else. I'm neutral. My father-in-law who is a war captain said he would like to get them initiated . . . so I go along with it to keep peace in the family anyway."

Powell was one of the two resident Navajos in the pueblo. I know of three others who had lived there in the past. Powell said that he had many friends at Isleta whom he had first met at AIS. There were "a few middle-aged" people here who didn't like Navajos, but he didn't know why. He had been in the kiva once to attend a ceremony where his wife's father took an active part. "They had a dance down there and so forth. I could have gone down before, but I'm just not interested. My wife wanted me to go because of her father so I went." Except for "christenings" he has little to do with those of the pueblo, including the other Navajo resident.

Powell's standard and style of living were quite different from that of the others at Isleta. His house had seven rooms: a large living room, a dining room, a kitchen, a bath, and three bedrooms. The walls were of thick adobe covered with a layer of stucco, and all floors were wooden. He had his own septic tank and a private well which supplied more than enough water. With the exception of the kitchen and bathroom, all rooms had wall-to-wall carpeting, and the furnishings were modern.

The family owned a stereo phonograph and a large TV set. The house was heated by butane gas, and Powell was in the process of installing air conditioning. He was an excellent craftsman and had built his home. When he and his wife first moved in, the place was in rather poor condition and probably resembled most of the other dwellings in the pueblo. He drove a new (1960) Chevrolet station wagon. His wife's kitchen was supplied with a wide variety of electrical appliances. She also had a large deep freeze unit well-stocked with meat. The yard surrounding the house was not planted in grass, and there was no garage.

Powell and his family dressed well. Most of their affluence was due to his salary, but his wife also worked full time as a receptionist in a dentist's office in Albuquerque.

Powell seemed to be leading a pleasant life. He described his daily routine:

Well, any normal day for me is getting up probably about 6:30 or a quarter to seven . . . and with the wife working I don't know when she gets up . . . I have to fix my own breakfast — a cup of coffee and a donut or something. Then I normally have a ride going into town if I work in town then I get to work around 8:00 o'clock, start off wherever I left off the previous day, depending on what I was doing. Then I have a coffee break about 10:00 o'clock or so, take about twenty minutes . . . and then go back to whatever we're doing and normally the days go pretty fast. Like I say it depends on what type of work I'm involved in at the time, and I don't take my lunch so I normally experiment with all the restaurants or places to eat. . . . We normally have another coffee break at 3:00 o'clock to kind of break up the day and get off at 5:00, and I usually catch a bus to where my wife works and I wait until she gets off and our baby sitter usually has supper ready for us about when we get home. The baby sitter is just a neighbor. She's a single woman. She stays and feeds the kids and leaves the supper on the table or in the stove for us and we're usually home by six or so, so we eat or read the paper and watch TV for a little while and then that's about the end of the day. . . . We're in bed by 9:00 o'clock and try to get the children in bed before that.

The whole family goes to a drive-in movie at least once a week, and they have taken short trips to such places as the Mescalero Reservation and Carlsbad Caverns on vacations. Powell occasionally reads "men's magazines" and *Life* and the *Reader's Digest*. He and his wife visit ten or twelve of his co-workers and their families about once a month:

It's mostly conversation, whatever might happen, dance or something and have something to eat, snacks and stuff. Take something some time and some beer or what you want to drink. They sit around and gossip.

Some associations are maintained by more indirect means:

We had to write about 200 Christmas cards last year, and we receive just about that amount too. You know once those things get started you almost gotta continue them because a guy will get mad at you if you don't send him one.

Powell hunts a great deal with his father-in-law and his brother who is working in Utah. They travel over most of New Mexico and Arizona after deer. The marshes and fields around his house are full of ducks and partridge.

His wife and children regularly attend the Catholic Church at the pueblo but Powell goes no more than once or twice a year.

His mother married a traditional Navajo and has had two daughters since Powell's father died. She was living at Rattlesnake. Powell and his wife last visited his mother in 1956. They attended a squaw dance for about an hour "but my wife didn't like it at all so we left." His mother calls him collect about once a month from a nearby trading post, but he makes no effort to contact her or any other relative on the reservation.

His children attend Albuquerque public schools. They are officially registered with the Navajo Tribe but only so that they may be eligible for the available material benefits. Navajos with a high school diploma are eligible to apply for a tribal college scholarship of $4,800. Albuquerque Navajo school children receive two complete outfits of clothing a year as do their counterparts on the reservation. Powell said that he had no interest in the reservation because "nothing that goes on out there could affect me." He has never voted in a local, tribal, state, or national election. However, he does vote in the annual pueblo election for governor and lieutenant-governor.

When I asked Powell what his central goals in life were, he replied: "Me, I gotta be financially situated and have a happy family and be satisfied with whatever I'm doing." He appears to have what he wants, and this situation will probably persist.

Joe Sandoval

Joe Sandoval was a thin, wan individual with a kind of personal intensity which penetrated the language barrier between us. He readily agreed to be an informant largely because of a remote kin tie with my interpreter which both recognized and honored. He was Tome's father's sister's daughter's divorced husband. As will be discussed below, he resented most Anglos and many "types" of Navajos. This resentment may have been positively correlated with his witch troubles. As Kluckhohn (1963: 85) has stated:

A . . . latent "function" of the corpus of witchcraft lore for individuals is that of providing a socially recognized channel for the expression (in varying degrees of obliquity) of the culturally disallowed. Certain aberrant impulses (such as those toward incest and necrophilia) may achieve some release in phantasy. . . .

Sandoval, like other traditionals whom I have known, gave relatively few details when asked to tell about his past life. Most of these data were recorded when we talked about traditional ceremonial practice, agriculture, and technology. Thus, the order of information found in this case history is mine, not his. This induced order is, however, necessary and not a distortion of the facts.

Sandoval is "forty or forty-two, I'm not sure which." His father was a conservative individual who had married two sisters. His mother, the younger, had three other sons and two daughters; Sandoval was the youngest boy. Five of his siblings had died when they were infants. His mother's father was an Anglo soldier who left the area before she was born. Joe's father, Nakai Sandoval, had a "Mexican" grandparent. This grandparent, Jose Sandoval, was a sometime tribal councilman.

It was Sandoval who told of his past life, but the English prose which follows is, of course, that of my interpreter.

I was born [circa 1920] in a kind of hogan near Red Rock that had the floor dug into the ground about five to six feet. I was born on a sheep skin. From since I was born we did all our singing ceremonials and had happiness and sadness as well in this hogan. It don't look like much but the people inside are very much alive. When I was three years old, I first remember that I have to behave according to what my father tells me. I guess that's the reason why I never went to school in those days. When I was five, I started herding the little rams. I guess every Navajo knows about taking care of the rams. The rams have to kept separate until breeding time in the fall. And then it's turned over with the rest of the flock. Then I herd the sheep all winter long. My job when I'm not doing those thing I have to take care of the horses. Until I became fifteen years old which was a very dull life. I didn't have no toys like some of the children today. We make our own toys, me and my brother. Then when I became fifteen years of age, I was more or less promoted doing a little bigger jobs such as breaking horses and taking care of wagons. Now and then I would herd the sheep. I felt that herding sheep was for the women. So I broke quite a few horses.

Sandoval was frail and sickly as a child. He had a number of sings and a great deal of additional exposure to traditional ceremonial practice. Such exposure was a pleasant and comforting experience. As he states:

They take the bull roarer outside and the first time in the east, then south, west and then north. When this is making all this noise, when it's in full tune it can be heard by *cheendi*, by coyotes, and all evil people. Even some of the witches probably hear that and then they know to stay away. I remember vividly years ago when I was very small I was told to go outside and take this bull roarer and I was scared until this bull roarer makes this roaring and I feel much better after that. It seems to have a psychological effect on me. When I get this bull roarer at that time and I make this roar and I go all away around the hogan, the corral and out to the horses, but I never did hit any [evil things] with it, not that I know of anyway.

Then when I was about twenty years of age I started going to the squaw dances and all the Navajo ceremonials and seeing the Navajo singers. And I guess you might say that I raised cain and there was nothing that I didn't do. Stealing horses, cars, all this I have done under the influence of liquor.

My interpreter who knew Sandoval about this time said:

Joe used to be very wild, he used too much whiskey and peyote. He would tell everybody that he was just going to the trading post for a couple of hours and then we wouldn't see him for a month. He used to run around in the winter without a coat on. When he came back from these little trips, he was half dead for a while.

This "wild" behavior may have stemmed from the fact that Sandoval's family suddenly lost most of their livestock about this time, supposedly because of the machinations of a witch. My interpreter described the situation as follows:

Sandoval's family has had a lot of trouble with witches, especially his oldest brother, George Hawk. Hawk was rather successful financially for a while and had over 1,000 head of sheep. Every spring and fall he had lots of cash [from the sale of wool in spring and lambs in the fall] and he always paid cash for a new pickup. All the men in the family would drive to Durango, Colorado, just to get beer. The brother started bragging a lot about his wealth and people in the neighborhood got jealous. His sheep started dying in bunches of twenty or thirty. They'd come down to the water hole and refused to move off and then die very soon. George started feeling funny and called in my father to ask him for advice. My father immediately realized that the loss

of sheep was the work of a witch. He told George to keep his mouth shut about being wealthy and maybe the witch would stop bothering him. By the next spring George was down to less than 100 sheep and he never was wealthy again. Joe was about sixteen or seventeen at the time. One day about then he was riding a horse down a twisting, rocky mountain trail. All at once he looked up and saw a witch sitting on a flat rock looking down at the area where Sandoval's family lived. The horse then fell and nearly killed him. Ever since then Joe has believed in witches. The witch was finally driven off by some kind of anti-witch ceremony.

Sandoval's family tried to divert him from these erring ways:

My folks tried to make a farmer out of me, and they told me to plant corn, melons and a lot of other things like the Anglo people do. They told me that the time was going to come where I was going to have to do these things.

Apparently their efforts along this line were unsuccessful. Sandoval wanted to become a singer but his drunken behavior made this impossible.

I really wanted to be a singer, I liked the "easy-come, easy-go" money, but after a while nobody would take me as an apprentice because my hands shook too much from drinking all that whiskey and wine. I couldn't make straight lines with the colors.

However, he associated as closely as he could with such activities.

I had the shongo [long hair worn in a knot on the back of the head] and wore beads around my neck on occasions like squaw dances and went to different sings. When you are singing or at a ceremonial all Navajos including the patient is dressed with a sweat band and beads around the neck. You wear red moccasins and have a mark on both sides of your cheek. This signifies that you are taking part in a sing. That's when I was really a Navajo when I wore that shongo on my head and wore the red moccasins.

Several times during my sessions with him Sandoval stated that traditional life had not provided the material wealth which he desired.

I always wanted lots of sheep, goats, and plenty of hard goods [silver and turquoise jewelry] but I never did get them. I guess I am a failure that way.

His family was too poor to afford the proper traditional wedding ceremony for him. He still resented this at the time I knew him.

We were married the Navajo way, yet we didn't have the full ceremony like old times. Sorta like elope. To get away from all the ceremony. I got married the Navajo way yet I didn't get the full treatment of the ceremonial. To go through the regular ceremonial for Navajo marriage you have to take your finger in this

huge dish of mush. You take some with your finger
and lick some off the south side first and then west,
north and east. Then maybe that's why I been sick all
my life because of that. The old time Navajos does that.
When it is my time to get married it was more or less
the short cut. They [his relatives] wanted this elope-
ment like thing that does away with all property
exchange.

Sandoval and his wife — Tome's cousin — had
three sons and a daughter in a hogan near Red
Rock at a place called "Cougar-Eats-the-Sheep."
Only the oldest son, Harry, survived. Sandoval said
nothing more about his wife, except that she divorced
him and is now living in Boulder, Colorado, with
their son. I know little of the details and the sequence
of events of this part of his life. His health continued
to be poor and he used peyote for a short time in a
fruitless effort to obtain relief. He continues:

With all this wrong doing that I've done plus breaking
horses and I been spilled by a lot of plow horses and
wild horses, somewhere I was injured. So I entered the
hospital at Shiprock for an examination in 1947 I
believe it was. They didn't say what I was sick from
but I was laid up in bed for two months. While I was
in bed, I wondered about the things that I had done.
Such as breaking horses, bull-dogging steers, roping and
branding cattle. Somewhere I must have strained my
lungs or liver. Something must have happened to me.
Which got me thinking all the way back. When you are
young like that you don't hesitate to jump on a bronco
like I did. Now I been laid up for about five months.
The doctors seem to think that my lung is somehow
rubbing my ribs which they thinks is TB. Then I was
taken to Albuquerque [to the TB sanatorium] in 1947
and I was about twenty-six years old. I stayed there
nine years.

After four years of complete bed rest Sandoval
was well enough to attend the sanatorium's school.
He had five years of studying, but learned very little.
He developed no facility for English. A successful
operation removed a diseased portion of one lung
and in 1956 he was discharged. His physician told
me that Sandoval had "arrested TB" but would
probably be able to lead a normal life if he got
enough rest and could have an adequate diet. Since
his family around Red Rock could not provide him
with either, he remained in Albuquerque working
at menial jobs. He drifted to Skid Row and was
soon drinking heavily. His renewed use of alcohol
may have been due to his extreme difficulties in
adjusting to urban life.

Another traditional Albuquerque Navajo, David
Hawkins, described his reaction to the city. His
feelings probably mirrored those of Sandoval.

If you never went to school, it's pretty hard to know
anyone. You know a person by how he dresses and if
he has a mustache that's what you call him. You don't
actually know his name. So it's pretty difficult for a
person like myself to get around the city, much less
speak English to people on the street. But all this when
a person is mad at you, if you don't understand him,
you can tell if he is mad at you, if you don't understand him, you can tell if he is mad. That's one thing
that don't change. There is several things that you just
learn from observation. The town the size of Albuquerque it's pretty hard for me to get around. You have to
learn to read and then learn to speak English and that
way you got to read these signs along the road. I always
wish I can read and speak the language. They just
have all kinds of writing all over the place and I can't
read it.... I can't even argue with a person because all
they say, they tell me to get out and I know what
they mean.

During the time Sandoval was hospitalized, he
came to realize — possibly with the help of a con-
scientious chaplain — that he was going to die
because he had led such a wicked life. He vowed
that if he recovered, he would become a Christian.

I know nothing of his activities during the first
few months after his release from the hospital except
for his consumption of liquor. Apparently he soon
came under the influence of the Christian missionaries working around the Skid Row area and was
induced to stop drinking. He became a Catholic,
then a Baptist. Tiring of this, and of his difficult
life in Albuquerque, he attended the Indian Bible
School at Cortez, Colorado. While he was here, he
learned how to "read" Navajo orthography and was
given a Bible written in Navajo. Armed with this,
he felt prepared to "preach the Gospel" to other
traditional Navajos.

As I have suggested elsewhere (1964: 79–93)
Sandoval and other Navajos like him are not true
converts to Christianity. Their interest in the faith, as
I interpret it, represents a mutual accommodation
of two qualitatively different systems — traditional
ceremonial practice and Christianity.

Sandoval ran away from the Bible School and
returned to Albuquerque. He worked as a silversmith at Maisels and later on at Bell's. He cheerfully
admitted that he was fired at both places because
he didn't work hard enough. In addition, the jobs
were rather dull and he didn't feel well. He then
found work running a dish-washing machine at a
plush motel. The pay wasn't much, but the work was
easy and there was always plenty of food around
to eat. While I knew him, he continued to work in
this capacity.

When I first met him, he was living in an unheated tool shed behind Henry Chavez's house. At that time he and Chavez were ardent Pentecostals. They had first become friends when they were both patrons of the Skid Row taverns. He took two of his meals with Chavez, but did not live in the house simply because there was no room.

The floor of the shed was covered with linoleum. An iron pipe clothes rack held approximately two dozen good quality sport shirts and slacks. Three Protestant religious calendars were on one wall. I noticed two radios. On top of a small chest of drawers a Navajo Bible and a prayer book were prominently displayed. A basketball ring was nailed to the wall over the bed. The place was very drafty and daylight showed through several cracks in one wall. At the other end of the narrow room were several coffee cans full of nails, bolts, and screws. On a narrow single bed there were several new, good quality blankets. A shaded light bulb hung from the ceiling. A battered rocking chair was drawn up close to the bed.

During my first winter in town Sandoval developed a serious chest cold from sleeping in the tool shed. He then moved into a shabby but warm room near the center of town.

A description of a married traditional family's home may serve as a basis of comparison with the dwelling of Joe Sandoval and round out the picture of the traditional Albuquerque Navajo. Jeff Morrison was a traditional and an ardent peyotist. His home consisted of a prefabricated three-room structure behind his employer's grocery store. The place was very clean but overcrowded. However, his wife and six children did not seem to mind. The floors were covered with new, well-waxed linoleum. The kitchen had an electric refrigerator, a gas stove, and a large sink with ample draining boards. Large cabinets were over the sink. The center of the room was occupied by a battered wooden table and four chairs. A disassembled loom was in one corner.

There was a single light bulb hanging from a cord in each room. The furniture in the living room was comprised of a 17-inch TV set, two radios (one a Zenith "Trans-Oceanic"), two overstuffed chairs, a tattered sofa, several Christian religious pictures, and two motto-signs, "Jesus never fails" and "God Bless Our Home." A Catholic crucifix hung on one wall. (I later asked Morrison why he kept Christian religious symbols around since he believed in the "old ways" and used peyote. He smiled and said

that these things had been given to him by missionaries and "peyote people don't hate nobody.")

The bedroom had two double beds and a fiber wardrobe closet. Covering most of two walls were recent photographs of reservation kinsmen and friends. All the traditional and some of the Anglo-modified Albuquerque Navajos had large collections of photographs of relatives and friends on the reservation prominently displayed in their homes. The permanent-resident Navajos did not.

Sandoval dressed well, according to traditional standards. His Levis were new, as were most of his other clothes. He wore well-polished Wellington boots and a good quality Stetson hat. He had a large silver Navajo belt buckle. Fastened to the back side of the buckle was an arrow point. The Franciscan Fathers (1910: 411) make the following comment on such use of arrow points:

. . . arrow-points are secured to a forelock of the patient in the course of some ceremonies. By some they are worn even after the ceremony, when the charm is . . . a mark indicative of a holy rite. According to ritual, small arrow-points to be worn as a charm must have been unearthed by a gopher.

Sandoval's daily routine would have been demanding for a healthy person. He must have regarded it as a burden.

I work at night, start work at 4:00 o'clock in the afternoon. One of the things about this job, I can get up any time in the morning I feel like — six, sometimes nine. It depends on the people who bang on my door in the morning [who were his traditional Navajo friends]. I get to work at 4:00 and run the dishwashing machine all the four hours until 8:00. Then we eat lunch. Then from 8:00 to 2:00, sometimes I stay there as long as 2:00 a.m., it depends how long it takes to wash the dishes. I generally get off at 12:30. Then I go home, and go to bed, I don't get a chance to watch TV or anything like that, because when I get off they're all closed and everybody's asleep. If I wander around at that hour I might get put in jail. I get up most of the time around 8:00 o'clock. After I get up I eat breakfast which takes one hour, by the time I walk down to the cafe. This cafe is next to the waiting place of the long dog. [Greyhound Bus Station] Then I see these people over at the Baptist Church. I go to school there from eleven to one most of the time last winter [to learn how to read and write English]. After I get off I go visit some of my friends or such people as Henry Chavez or Dan Sanders [a Navajo and co-worker at the motel kitchen]. Then I eat dinner or lunch at Dan's place or at Henry's. And at 2:00 I'm going to work, because I have to catch a bus to Wyoming Street so I can walk only five miles to work. . . . Sometimes when I get off work I catch a ride back here but mostly I don't. When I walk back [approximately fifteen miles]

I generally am in the house about two or three in the morning.

His contacts with others seemed to be limited.

If I have to walk home all the way from Western Skies Motel I have no energy left to go around visiting everybody. I stay in and rest most of the day. My friends come around here about twice a week to visit me, and Henry come to see me about once a week. I go over there about once a week to see him. But I see most of these people every Sunday at church. [an all-Navajo Pentecostal Church located just north of Isleta Pueblo] But some of these people [traditional Navajos living in town] they never come around to visit me. They know where I live but they just don't want to be bothered. The only time a lot of these people visit me is when they want to borrow something. The other people around here the neighbors [who are Anglo], they just speak to me but I never visit them.

Sandoval tried to visit the reservation at least once a month, but this was difficult to do in the winter because of the poor reservation roads. When he could get a ride to Red Rock with a friend, he visited as many relatives as he could and spent quite a bit of time talking with the old people "because they know the right way how to live and to do things right." He had no contact with his former wife and son.

The necessity of trying to live in a traditional and Anglo urban world had been a harsh experience for him. His perception of some Anglos and Navajos reflected this bitter struggle.

From the beginning the wine and whiskey was brought into this country by the Anglos which seems to me that this was much wrong doing. Just like giving dope to teen-agers. My friends on the reservation ask me, they often wonder how we live in the city with all this hurry-hurry. Have to be at a certain time, a certain place which to my people this way of living is fantastic, you can't afford to make mistakes in this place [the city].

There is a lot of Navajo that neglects their family, that's supposed to be looking for a job off the reservation, then you hear about them in Santa Fe in the state pen there. And here's another bad Navajo. He make a lot of money off the reservation, he gets pay several hundred dollars in ready cash, he has a few drinks, he sounds worse than the Texans. Finally another Navajo tell him to shut up. By doing this he gets in a fight with this character and they both go to jail by the time the day is over and it takes all their money to pay the fines to get out, which is down-right stupid I agree. The next morning he has hangover and he says 'What happen?' Then he hears, 'Your fine was this much.' Then he brags about how much he paid. But worst of all kind of Navajo is the witches.

Sandoval's fear of witches was well-founded. In May of 1960, while sleeping in a car at Canyoncito after an evening of Gospel preaching, he said he was attacked.

I been asleep about two hours. Suddenly a tapping on the car and a cold wind [the car windows were closed] woke me up. The car started to shake. My mind felt small and it was being dragged away. I hollered out 'Jesus and God' as loud as I could for several times. Finally everything stopped and the witch went away. I still feel sick. I'm going to have to go to the reservation for a sing.

Sandoval's average annual earnings of $1,200 provided him with the essentials of life in an urban setting, but allowed him few luxuries. He attempted to buy a secondhand car on the installment plan, but lost it after a few months because of his failure to make the payments. His chief pleasure seemed to be taking part in Pentecostal Church services and discussing "the Gospel" with his Navajo associates. I believe that he also gained a certain measure of solace from this. He also enjoyed "going to the great big sweat house [steam room] at Vic Tanney's Gym."

This sweat house is much better than the kind that they have on the reservation. In this one you could even dance around while you are inside. I really think that the tribal council should build a lot of these for people out on the reservation.

After fifteen months contact with him, I had the strong impression that he regarded urban residence as nothing more than a painful necessity. The only aspects of the Anglo world which he valued were medical practices, "but only for the Anglo kind of diseases," and a few technological developments such as cars and TV. His orientation was toward the traditional reservation although he was interested in the Tribal Council politics at Window Rock. He felt that his doctor at the sanatorium really didn't understand his illness as well as a singer would. This was why he was still sick.

As soon as he "felt better" he wanted to return permanently to the reservation and have "lots of horses and sheep and a big irrigated farm." However, he realized that he would probably never have these things.

The Navajo way is the best. All a Navajo wants out of life is living. He should live on his land in pride and dignity, as tall as a pine tree. But I will never have land. In about twenty years I can see myself back around Red Rock just chopping wood and things like that.

Sandoval frequently commented that "you can't live the Anglo way and the Navajo way at the same time." His life was an eloquent testimonial to the validity of this fact.

From the material presented, one might get the impression that Sandoval was a cynical, embittered individual, but this is only partially true. Despite his difficulties he seemed to have an admirable zest for living. He was an excellent teller of myths, and he could make such figures as Coyote, Changing Woman, and Big Monster assume a vividness that is impossible for me to describe. While he mistrusted and feared many "types" of Anglos and Navajos, he recognized that both races also had desirable "types" of people. Subjectively, I would say that most of the time he was a Navajo who "walked in Beauty."

Joseph Barnes

Joseph Barnes was a short and rather nervous person. He was very willing to work with me, and I recorded more data in eight hours from him than from any other Navajo in Albuquerque. Unlike Powell and Sandoval, however, he failed to discuss the painful events of his life in any detail. Much of the data he supplied concerns his association with the traditional aspects of Navajo life. He spoke of these things with an obvious relish and satisfaction.

Barnes was born in 1933 near Tohatchi, the youngest son of the family. His preschool years were spent in the winter "down in the flat country below Chuska Mountain." During the warmer months he stayed in a summer camp near the crest of Chuska Peak established at a place called "the arrow was uprooted by water," because "there was always enough water and grass there for all the sheep we had then."

His mother died when he was two. An infant sister died shortly afterwards. His father showed little interest in his family and was mainly concerned with a pick-up truck and the consumption of wine and whiskey. Accordingly, he "was with my mother's side most of the time." His mother's sister "Aunt Charlotte," his mother's parents Many Horses Barnes and Old Charlotte, and Old Charlotte's sister, Mrs. Smith, were the most prominent adults during his childhood. His mother's younger brothers, Willie, Harry, Deswood, and Nealwood, two of his second wife's brothers, Everett and Johnny, and his own

brother Eddie, were his principal companions. All of these people were traditional and spoke no English. Barnes did not meet a non-Navajo until he entered the government boarding school at Tohatchi when he was about six.

These years were generally satisfying ones for him. "My Aunt Charlotte, she sing me songs I never hear any more." During the periods when the adults had little to do, they told him of the events of their early years, 1864–1900. A Ute raiding party once attacked the sheep camp about 1900, but was driven off with the loss of two of its members. "Old Charlotte, she caught one and choked him to death by stuffing sand in his mouth." About this time two Anglos had stolen some horses from another Navajo sheep camp nearby. "Many Horses Barnes and his father Many Horses, they and lots of others found them and beat them to death with big rocks. They was awful glad about that." Barnes also heard in great detail of the Long Walk to Fort Sumner and how some of his elders had escaped from federal troops and hidden alone in the mountains in small groups for the four years, 1864–68.

When he was about five, he began to herd sheep.

The way I took care of them was in the morning take them out of corral there, this would be in summer camp, we start to look for good pasture land for the day. Take them out there and just try to keep them all together. Not have any strays. Have to keep coyotes away. I move around the circle of the whole herd, every ten to fifteen minutes anyway. Maybe sing to them. Then at end of day keep track, count up, make sure none gone. It was monotonous. I was out there all by myself most of time anyway.

This theme of loneliness is prominent in all of the life stories of the Anglo-modified Navajos. Roger Ball was more articulate about this:

Early in the fall, my folks, the whole family left for piñon picking. They left me all alone. Of course, I was pretty lonesome. I was a lonely boy . . . at night I be so scared. I build great big fire in hogan . . . Sometimes I climb up in tree on top of high hill. I climb up this and climb in tree and look where my folks went. I sit up there and cry. I was just that lonely.

When Barnes was six, Aunt Charlotte and Mrs. Smith took him and his brother to school at Tohatchi. He had one of the first baths of his life, was given some overalls, and placed in a large room "with many toys." Like John Powell he enjoyed the classroom work, but hated the discipline. All children were forced to go to church. Early Sunday morning all the boys were marched to a store room where they put on "their" suits. Immediately after church they were marched back and exchanged the suits for overalls. The meals at the school must have been inadequate because Barnes mentioned how on several different occasions he and other students had broken into food storage cellars "and then we really ate good." During his first school year Barnes' class was taken to see a circus in Gallup. They enjoyed the circus but found Gallup frightening.

Barnes' interest in traditional Navajo life persisted and he often ran away from school "but only on weekends" to watch Many Horses Barnes work as a singer. He attended at least "two dozen" sings. His interest was heightened when his mother's brothers became assistants. He was usually barred from most of this activity because "they kept telling me little kids shouldn't get too close to something like that." Since he was away at school during the winter, he missed learning many details of ceremonial lore since traditionals feel that the latter can be discussed safely only after the crops have been harvested and before spring planting has begun. One of his favorite pastimes at school was playing "Black Jacks" with his friends, a game which Aunt Charlotte had taught him. When he went back to the sheep camp in the summer of 1940, he again herded sheep and began going to squaw dances and playing "the shoe game."

The effects of the stock reduction program were experienced later by his family than by Navajos living in other areas of the reservation. This may be due to the fact that his family lived in a relatively isolated area, and Navajos living in the northeast portion of the reservation resisted stock reduction more successfully than did Navajos living elsewhere. About this time the Federal Government took the majority of the livestock owned by Many Horses Barnes. The BIA fined his relatives, but they were not treated as sternly as the families of many of my Anglo-modified informants. In some cases the flocks of these families were driven into trenches, saturated with gasoline, and burned alive.

During this summer his Aunt Charlotte died of tuberculosis. Several of the family had the disease, but she was the first to die. Barnes' father appeared at the funeral and succeeded in getting his son "half drunk" on cheap wine.

For the next five years his life fell into the routine of attending school in the winter and working around the sheep camp in summer. Barnes continued to enjoy school and found working in the carpentry shop especially satisfying. When he was about nine or ten, his grandfather started to teach him the medicinal and ceremonial uses of many wild plants and herbs. At that time he became convinced that "these things really work and there is something to these old ways."

In 1944 Many Horses Barnes and his sons, Willie, Harry, Deswood, and Nealwood, went to California to work as laborers. However, Willie got into trouble "and it took all of their money to get him out of jail, so they just came right back." Barnes thought that this incident was very funny.

In 1945, when he was twelve, Barnes started going to the Catholic Mission School at St. Michaels. By this time he played poker quite well, and found the game to be exceptionally lucrative when he cheated. With the ten dollars he had "won" from his inept but honest companions at the sheep camp, he was able to purchase most of his school supplies.

But it really turned out all right, because the next time me and them boys went into Gallup on a Saturday, I paid their way to this show and got some candy too. They just couldn't figure out why I was so nice to them.

Barnes was soon made a Catholic and must have impressed the good Fathers as being unusually pious because he was made an altar boy. He found this role rather irksome until one day before Mass he drank a bottle of wine intended for Communion. "That was about the funniest thing I ever done. And they never did find out that I done it."

His classroom study continued to go well and he was allowed to skip two grades of work. He spent some time in a hospital at Fort Defiance because he was suspected of having heart trouble and trachoma.

When he came back to the sheep camp in 1946, he found the area to be very depressing:

Everything was real bad. People weren't friendly no more. There wasn't no food much. Before you could just go around to where anybody was livin' and they'd be eating and give you all you wanted, but then they just ate at meal times and wouldn't eat at all if you was there. Nobody had much sheep, not much money either.

This condition could have been the result of the loss of war-time wage work. This loss was a hardship to many areas of the reservation.

In 1947 when he was fourteen, he was sent to the Indian School in Albuquerque. He learned to get around the city within a month and apparently had no unpleasant experiences doing so. He enjoyed the classes and soon told one of his teachers that he wanted to go to college.

After the first year's work at Albuquerque, he returned home to the sheep camp which was now located in the southern part of the Lukachukai Mountains. He got "awful drunk" from drinking a bottle of wine and some "Four Rose" whiskey supplied by Deswood. His grandparents were amused by this but insisted that he continue herding sheep. He returned to Albuquerque in the fall. He spent most of the next summer picking peaches in southwestern Colorado because his family had no livestock left and there were few crops to cultivate.

He also worked eleven days as a laborer for a railroad in this state, but soon had to quit because one of the railroad unions went on strike. He was then seventeen and showed a great deal of self-reliance and endurance. He had traveled alone by bus from Gallup to Colorado, and then walked several miles at night to the railroad siding where several hundred other Navajos were living in converted box cars. After going without sleep for thirty-six hours, he put in a full day's work laying new track ties.

Soon after Sandoval returned to AIS in the fall, his grandfather, Many Horses Barnes, was critically injured in a car accident. Barnes and his brother returned briefly to the reservation just before he died.

The summer before his senior year in high school, Barnes worked for a florist in Albuquerque doing menial tasks and making flower arrangements.

During his senior year he applied to a small liberal arts college for a scholarship and to the Tribal Council for an educational loan. (Tribal college scholarships were not offered until 1954.) Neither was granted although the faculty of AIS thought highly of him. References in his file are, in part, as follows:

Pleasant to work with and applies himself to his work. . . . Absolutely dependable, hard working, cooperative and capable of independent work. . . . If he has any failing it would be that of acting too impulsively without thinking before hand. Good powers of organization, absolutely honest. Pronounced stammer when excited. Despite his mildness of manner, and slightness of figure, he has guts.

He was valedictorian of his class.

He returned to the reservation but came back to Albuquerque in a few days because "there was nothing there, just nothing." I pressed for his reasons for staying around Albuquerque. He replied:

Maybe I just wanted to get away from herding sheep. I never did know what keep me here except maybe it was that summer working for the florist. I liked the job and being here in town.

When he got back to town, he tried to enlist in the Air Force, but was rejected because of ingrown toe nails. He had this condition remedied but decided not to enlist. He saw an opening advertised in the paper for a delivery boy at a local paint and glass company and applied for the job. He was accepted but then realized that he had no driver's license and didn't know how to drive. By spending a week observing the Anglo college boy he was replacing, he learned how to handle the delivery truck. About a year later he acquired a driver's license.

In September, 1952, by "acting too impulsively" he got Georgia, a Navajo girl from his graduating class, pregnant. At this time he had been living with another single Navajo boy in Albuquerque. After they discovered her pregnancy, Barnes and Georgia rented a small dingy apartment and started housekeeping. Barnes kept his job with the paint company. The following January the school authorities learned of the situation and wrote to Georgia's parents who were living near Crownpoint asking for permission for them to marry. This was apparently granted. In May, 1953, Georgia died giving birth to their son. Her parents took the baby and Joseph never saw him.

In 1954, Barnes married a girl who was also a classmate and had grown up near his grandparents' sheep camp. They were married by a Justice of the Peace.

By 1956 they had two sons and two daughters. Barnes had been promoted to the post of bookkeeper with the paint company. In the spring of this year Barnes was found to have tuberculosis and spent about eight months in a sanatorium. Shortly thereafter his wife was also sent there. Their children were placed in foster homes in Gallup.

When he was discharged from the hospital, Barnes returned to the paint company and acted as an assistant manager of one store. When his wife recovered, their children were returned to them. In 1960 they bought a new five room house and life had settled into a regular pattern for them.

He describes his daily routine:

Well, during the winter months, I would get up around seven and then I would rush to get to leave home about seven thirty. Sometime I have breakfast, sometime I don't. Then pick up mail and go to work and take care of sales at the store all day, have lunch at the store, and then get back home at five thirty. Then have supper and then we be around here or go down to shop, or run errands, and have the kids in bed around nine and then stay up until ten or ten thirty.

Barnes probably didn't make more than $6,000 to $6,500 a year, but he had most of the desirable material things which prosperous urban living could provide. His frame stucco house was new and located in a pleasant suburban neighborhood. He had a combination bath and shower. His wife used a new electric stove and had many electric utensils. His house had central heating, and the furnishings were new. In the living room, a large, round, green rug lay on a highly polished waxed floor, and a low sofa and two easy chairs furnished one-half of the room. In the center was a glass-covered cocktail table flanked by a 21-inch TV set. There were two radios and a phonograph. A cuckoo clock and two very trite prints hung on the wall. I didn't see the other rooms but assume that they were furnished in a similar style. Barnes had a new car.

During hours of relaxation, reading was confined to mysteries, the daily paper, and a few popular magazines such as *Look, Catholic Digest, Kiplinger Report, and* the *Saturday Evening Post.* For entertainment Barnes frequently attended the local minor league baseball games and an occasional wrestling match. In the winter he did some league bowling. He had no interest in local, state, or federal politics and seldom voted in a national election. He and his wife voted in the tribal election. His wife often "had coffee" with other neighborhood housewives.

The family seemed to have few contacts with others. One or two of his co-workers who were "Spanish" visited him about once a year, and their visits were reciprocated with equal frequency. Their closest contacts were with his wife's sister and her Navajo husband who was an office manager for a large furniture store. Both families helped each other by babysitting and fending off relatives from the reservation.

Barnes belonged to the Navajo Club and a smaller Indian organization. His wife and children went to the Catholic Church but he did not. The Barneses visited his relatives on the reservation about three or four times a year during the summer. They usually visited her relatives once a year. Relatives called collect once a month asking for money. Barnes did not say whether or not they gave them money.

He had no contact with his classmates from AIS who were still living in town.

The family dressed well. Barnes and his wife spoke Navajo in their home only when they wanted to "keep secrets" from their children. The children were not learning Navajo.

Barnes had hoped to have a small paint and glass store of his own, but even if he could have had his own business he felt it would not be especially appealing, for very little money could be made. Also, since he had mastered all the tasks involved in such a business, it was no longer viewed by him as desirable.

Now [after seven years of experience] I mix paint, cut glass, wait on people, keep books, just as well as anybody. Nothing more to learn. I'm an old hand now. But I don't know. The way it's going there's nothing more to learn. It was interesting to me. I never did keep track of time before until just lately anyways where it seem like now everything slowing down. I don't see any more promotion at least nothing more unless we set up some more dealers here in town or around the state.

Soon after we finished work, Barnes was passed over for a new dealership, and the position was given to an Anglo. This action may or may not have been justified. He had also developed a skin allergy to paint fumes.

Barnes said that he would go back to the reservation if he could work for the tribe, and "live right" but there were very few jobs and currently these were filled. He thought that the reservation might be abolished in fifteen or twenty years, so perhaps such a job, even if it were available, might not have much future. He also said that when he did see his relatives, they told him that he was no longer a Navajo because "he lived like an Anglo." Just before I left Albuquerque he asked me if I thought it would be possible for him to open a bowling alley on the reservation, preferably at Window Rock. I could not answer this question.

As I finished the last session, he commented: "You know, if I hadn't gone to school, I wouldn't know about all this [urban life with its rewards, disappointments, and annoyances]. I'd probably be still living out there with all my relatives." I seriously doubt if he could decide whether his current status was a blessing or a curse.

Barnes' great-great-great-grandfather was Manuelito, one of the last Navajo war chiefs and a prominent figure after the return from Fort Sumner. Shortly before he died, he made the following statement (Underhill 1953: 4) to interpreter Chee Dodge who later became chairman of the Tribal Council:

My grandchild, the whites have many things which we Navajos need. But we cannot get them. It is as though the whites were in a grassy canyon and there they have wagons, plows, and plenty of food. We Navajos are up on the dry mesa. We can hear them talking but we cannot get to them. My grandchild, education is the ladder. Tell our people to take it. . . .

I wonder if Manuelito would say the same thing today if he could know the fate of one of his descendants.

SUMMARY AND CONCLUSIONS

This chapter has examined the structure and operation of the urban-reservation system. Common background and foreground factors for sixteen Navajos have been presented in an attempt to suggest some prominent characteristics associated with each of the three orientations. Detailed material consisting of condensed life histories and current patterns of urban living for three individuals exemplifying the three orientations has been offered. It is evident from the data given in this latter section that these three Navajos are generally representative of their categories.

6. CONCLUSIONS AND SUGGESTIONS FOR ADDITIONAL RESEARCH

CONCLUSIONS

The data supplied in the body of this study generally confirm the hypotheses presented in the introductory chapter. More extensive research on the Albuquerque Navajos or Navajos living in other urban centers might or might not lead to their modification.

Isolation of common characteristics of sixteen Navajos, plus intensive study of three additional individuals, has confirmed and justified the classification of the Albuquerque Navajos into three basic cultural orientation groups: permanent-resident, Anglo-modified, and traditional. The basic attributes which delineate these categories have been repeatedly exhibited by individuals classified within them. The postulated dynamics of the urban-reservation system have been demonstrated.

Few Navajos want to live permanently in Albuquerque because the city, and in all probability urban residence per se, cannot provide them with a style of living which they regard as desirable and necessary. For the Anglo-modified Navajos such a desirable and necessary existence consists of access to a maximum level of Anglo technology utilized in a transitional reservation community. Traditional Navajos would require a much lower level of Anglo technology, perhaps limiting themselves to pick-up trucks, firearms, and certain items of clothing such as boots, Stetson hats, jeans, and blankets. In contrast to their Anglo-modified tribesmen, they want to live in a traditional reservation community. Both Anglo-modified and traditional Navajos want to escape from the city's rapid pace of living, impersonal relationships, and general competitive tone.

Permanent-resident Navajos not only accept these aspects of living, but desire them. To the traditional and Anglo-modified Navajos they are still regarded as fellow tribesmen, but they are viewed as "Navajos-who-live-and-act-like-Anglos." It is not known how Anglos, "Spanish," and other Indians regard the permanent-resident Navajos, and, in particular, if they make a distinction between permanent-resident, Anglo-modified, and traditional residents.

In addition to the confirmation of the major and ancillary hypotheses, several other general conclusions can be made concerning Albuquerque Navajos. The large majority of Albuquerque's Navajos lead quiet, productive lives and must be regarded as good citizens by any sort of objective standards of evaluation. Most Navajos live harmoniously with non-Navajo residents and have many Anglo and "Spanish" friends and associates. Navajos have demonstrated virtually from the city's birth that they are as capable of successful urban adaptation as are the non-Navajo occupants in that they can utilize the city's economic, medical, recreational, and other facilities as well as the residents of other ethnic classifications.

Most of the 275 Navajos studied closely resemble other Albuquerque Indians and non-Indian residents in their general patterns of living, such as house type, manner of dress, language use, and an adherence to a daily routine of regular meals, working hours and rest, and recreational habits. Those not conforming to these general patterns are the few prostitutes and the traditionals.

It should be emphasized here that most conclusions which this analysis has produced apply only to the 275 Navajos who lived in Albuquerque during the period of my residence there. Generalizations of much wider scope might be premature.

The comparative data concerning off-reservation Navajos outside of Albuquerque are fragmentary and uneven. Hence, an extensive comparison with the Albuquerque material is unwarranted, although some comment can be made. The Albuquerque

Navajos in many respects do not resemble the seasonal off-reservation Navajos. There is the obvious difference in modes of residence. The seasonal workers appear to be closely tied to the traditional economic cycle of the reservation. Temporary off-reservation residence, which usually involves residence in migrant labor camps and/or converted railroad box cars, is a situation far different from city living. These seasonal workers differ from the Albuquerque Navajos in that they have a reasonably adequate and satisfactory living base on the reservation. The Albuquerque Navajos lack this, which is one of the main reasons why they are living in town.

Albuquerque Navajos resemble Navajo residents in other cities in that they conform to common traditional, Anglo-modified, and permanent-resident living patterns.

Navajos in a given city do not form a cohesive group, but rather constitute an aggregate of migrants who have little or nothing to do with each other. At times deliberate avoidance and animosity may exist between Navajo individuals and families. Most Navajos now living in cities want eventually to return to the reservation.

For reasons discussed elsewhere there are probably few permanent-resident Navajos in any city. There may or may not be significant differences between Navajos living in towns near the borders of the reservation and those living in cities some distance away. Parker (1954) notes that some Farmington Navajos have left livestock and jewelry with their kinsmen living back on the reservation. I found no evidence of such a practice among the Albuquerque Navajos.

Some Navajos may prefer to live in a reservation border town rather than in a city which is much farther away from their homes, but this is not certain. Albuquerque (1960) has a total population of about 200,000, but only 275 of this number are Navajos. The Gallup area has a total population of about 14,000, with an Indian population of 5,500, most of which is Navajo. Does this mean that for a Navajo residence in Gallup is preferable to residence in Albuquerque? This question cannot be answered here.

With equal logic, it can be suggested that there may be Navajos who want to live as far away from the reservation as possible. My interpreter's brother is a civil engineer who lives in Dallas. When I asked him if he would like to live in Albuquerque, he replied:

Dallas is just fine because any closer [to Shiprock] than this and I'm too near all my kin folks. This is close enough to get back in a hurry if there is an emergency, but far enough away so that most of my relatives can't bother me.

It seems reasonable to suggest that different sorts of urban communities may constitute qualitatively different types of off-reservation niches. A traditional Navajo living in the mining town of Rico does not have the same kind of life that a traditional Navajo does in Albuquerque. Unfortunately, this question cannot be considered here with any precision.

SUGGESTED AVENUES FOR ADDITIONAL RESEARCH ON URBAN INDIANS

Several avenues for additional research regarding urban Indians stem from this study. Before considering them, it is necessary to answer this basic question: What is the central contribution of this study? In my opinion, its primary contribution is the presentation of organized descriptive materials within a problem framework. Such data are currently lacking for reasons discussed in the introduction. The existence of this preliminary analysis will make future research on urban Indians of immediate interest to anthropologists, sociologists, and economists. Public administrators, social workers, and employees of the Bureau of Indian Affairs will also find the data to be of practical value. However, the preliminary study is directed primarily toward the field of anthropology.

The question of *what* should be done is closely related to the complementary question of *why* a particular line of study should be followed. The suggestions offered below attempt to answer both questions. Only suggestions of a very general nature are presented. Specific suggestions for further research have been made at various intervals throughout this study.

It is asserted that descriptive material, if comprehensive enough to include the basic categories of standard ethnographic inquiry, is of value in itself since it is a prerequisite to "the ultimate task of the anthropological enterprise . . . to explain the uniformities and diversities in the natural condition of mankind." (Goldschmidt 1959: 31). Since so little effort has been devoted to describing urban Indians, additional systematic description is certainly warranted.

The general purpose of this study, viewed in its broadest perspective, has been to explore in a limited fashion the relationship between migration and behavior. The Navajo reservation-urban migration provides a detailed and specific case study.

This instance of migration has simultaneous reflections on at least three levels: first, the general American urban migration which is conceived as a product of the contraction of the rural economy and the expansion of its urban counterpart; second, the general American Indian migration pattern; and third, the general, world-wide process of the dynamics of enclaves. Since the fact of urban migration by Indians is a part of a much wider population movement, its study can make a significant contribution to the area of inter-cultural relations. When members of a rural-based population move into an urban environment, which aspects of their former behavior do they retain? What aspects are subject to change? Of course, these questions have been given considerable attention in the past by such important figures as Tonnies, Maine, Morgan, and Redfield. However, the examination of additional illustrative material may yield new insights into this general problem.

Many anthropologists today are concentrating on more complex and realistic units for study rather than the single "isolated" culture in favor thirty years ago. As Lesser (1961: 42–3) has said:

I propose to ask what difference it makes if we adopt as a working hypothesis the universality of human contact and influence — as a fundamental feature of the socio-historical process; if we conceive of human societies — prehistoric, primitive, or modern — not as closed systems, but as open systems; if we think of any social aggregate not as isolated, separated by some kind of wall, from others, but as inextricably involved with other aggregates, near and far, in weblike, netlike connections. . . .

The concept of social field, or field of social relations, being developed and used by British social anthropologists — Firth, Fortes, Gluckman, Barnes, among others — seems to fit the realities of socio-historical human situations, so described. Firth has put it concisely: "Fields of social relations, not clear-cut societies, must be the more empirical notion of social aggregates." In this discussion I suggest the concept be understood in the sense of Durkheim's statement of many years ago: "There is no people and no state which is not part of another society, more or less unlimited, which embraces all the peoples and all the states with which the first comes in contact, either directly or indirectly."

The Navajo urban-reservation system presented here is one such example. Obviously only rudimentary consideration has been given to this system or field, and only a superficial understanding of its operation has been gained. An adequate examination would include a thorough understanding of the reservation communities and the place of various individuals within them. A careful study of the various niches which Navajos occupy in the city is also required. Much more should be known about the forces which operate between the reservation and urban orbits. It is also necessary to determine whether or not it is possible to refer to an urban-reservation system, or if it is necessary to recognize several systems varying in nature with the particular reservations and cities involved.

Finally, it is argued that an inter-disciplinary approach must be applied if the full significance of rural Indians in urban settings is to be grasped. Economics, sociology and geography can make vital contributions to such an endeavor. As Gluckman (1964: 158–261) suggests, such an approach must be used with caution, but the probable results outweigh the necessary difficulties involved.

APPENDIX I
FIELD METHODS

No doubt it is a high satisfaction to behold various countries and the many races of mankind, but the pleasures gained at the time do not counterbalance the evils. It is necessary to look forward to a harvest, however distant that may be, when some fruit will be reaped, some good effected.

Charles Darwin.
The Voyage of the Beagle, p. 498

A brief discussion of field methods is important since they are a means of assessing the validity and reliability of the data and because relatively little work has been done by anthropologists on urban American Indians. Some techniques are used which are not required in traditional field work. A discussion of the use and effectiveness of the techniques which I employed may be of interest to those contemplating similar research.

The opportunity to study urban Navajos in Albuquerque developed unexpectedly, so that little preparation through reading or talking to those who had worked with Navajos was possible. Such initial ignorance did have its advantages insofar as I was burdened unduly with preconceptions regarding Navajo culture. No specific problem was formulated prior to going to the field, and work began only with the intention of gathering as much data on as many aspects of urban Navajo life as was possible. The gathering of data was divided into initial, middle, and final phases.

In the initial phase — August to November, 1959 — I read the available literature on Navajos and the Southwest, became oriented in Albuquerque, took a census of the Navajo population there, and learned a smattering of the Navajo language. At the end of this period, a general acquaintance had been made with approximately eighty Navajos.

As soon as I arrived in Albuquerque, a local sociologist spent a few hours driving me around the city. He then suggested that I contact the president of the Navajo Club, Walter Higgins. I told Higgins that I was interested in studying urban Navajos since the results of such study might well help reservation Navajos coming to Albuquerque and other urban areas in the future to cope with the problems of city living. He readily agreed to cooperate and suggested that I begin attending the monthly Navajo Club meetings.

At the first meeting, I introduced myself to the group as an anthropologist who would like to learn something about Navajos in cities. I told them that I was also interested in learning the language and would be willing to pay for instruction. After the formal part of the meeting was over, two Navajos introduced themselves and agreed to help me in my language studies. Bob Elliot was in his forties; he worked only part of the time because of poor health. He had worked with anthropologists before and was rather conservative in outlook. Marshall Tome worked for a local newspaper and seemed eager to be of service. He had also worked previously with other anthropologists.

During this introductory period I had five one-hour sessions a week with Elliot and two evening periods a week with Tome. Some knowledge of the language was acquired, but much more was learned about local Navajos and Navajo culture in general. Elliot asked for $1.00 a session. Tome refused any pay. Since he was relatively prosperous, pressing payment seemed a little silly. Elliot returned permanently to the reservation in January. Tome soon was working with me six to eight hours a week and continued to do so until I left. I continued to attend club meetings throughout my stay.

The Navajo Tribe permits its people to vote by absentee ballot in its election for council chairman and vice-chairman. Since there had been an election the previous year, Walter Higgins gave me the voting registration list for Albuquerque. I began calling upon those listed in the evenings, and averaged about three or four meetings a week. The reservation and Albuquerque Navajo situations were discussed in general. Fewer than six people refused to see me. I attribute this generally favorable response to the courtesy, openness, and curiosity of the Navajos.

Soon after my arrival, I also contacted two Mormon elders who had been assigned to do mission work with the local Indians. Throughout my stay we exchanged information about Navajos. With the aid of these missionaries, my interpreters, and other Navajos I attempted to define the perimeters of my universe. I am reasonably sure that I acquired a good working knowledge of the local Navajo inhabitants. By October, 1959, I had a roster of 220 names. My efforts to add to this list continued throughout my stay, but only 55 additions could be made. Most of these were Navajos who came to the city after October.

While most Navajos contacted were courteous and many agreed to assist me to the point of inconvenience, I was accepted as a friend by only one Navajo, Marshall Tome. I suspect that most Navajos felt too uncomfortable as informants to regard me as anything more than a source of information regarding other Navajos and a comical distraction when I tried to speak their language. In the final months of my work, several of the traditional Navajos used me as an interpreter of aspects of urban Anglo living which puzzled them. These included such things as beatniks, alimony, and "conspicuous consumption for status emulation."

The middle phase of my work — November to December 1959 — was spent in considering what kinds of data were available to me, and how I might go about gathering them. My chief difficulties centered around the effectiveness of my interpreters in dealing with non-English-speakers and the distressing fact that those Navajos who were willing to cooperate had very little time to do so. During the initial phase I used four interpreters, but soon relied upon only one, Marshall Tome. My first interpreter, Bob Elliot, asked the non-English-speakers only questions that he was interested in. His English was rather poor and much of what he learned could not be communicated to me. He also resented my using other interpreters because he regarded this as a loss of income. Woody Carlson was an alert and willing interpreter but his Navajo was very poor. Many of my traditional informants

refused to work with him after a time. Roger Ball had only a moderate command of Navajo and an indifferent grasp of English. Much of his time working with me he spent in discussing the alleged imperfections of the current Tribal Council administration with non-English-speakers.

Marshall Tome was a capable interpreter, willing to gather the data that I wanted. He also made very helpful suggestions in extending and clarifying many areas of inquiry. He successfully maintained a neutral position in the dispute between the advocates and enemies of the Tribal Council. He was made even more acceptable to the other Albuquerque Navajos because his father was a highly respected and admired outfit leader and a sometime tribal councilman. He had, from my point of view, two shortcomings: First, because of the demands of his job and family, he, like most Albuquerque Navajos, could not work more than two hours at a time, and this was usually in the evening; second, he was highly ambivalent about peyote. The peyotists spoke little or no English. Hence, I could learn relatively little about the peyotists and could not attend services because of lack of an interpreter. A close association with peyotists, however, might have made me unacceptable to other Navajos. Tome was by far the best available interpreter, and I stopped using the other three Navajos after November, 1959.

Since my sessions were so limited in time, I decided, with my informants' permission, to tape record all formal sessions. Of course, conversations held while "pub-crawling," after Navajo Club meetings and at other informal times were not recorded. Most telephone conversations were not recorded. All Navajos approved of the use of the tape recorder because it made possible the fast and accurate collection of data. The non-English-speakers especially appreciated its use because it obviated the necessity of an immediate translation of material, a practice which they regarded as very "boring." Once my interpreter and I became known and accepted by a non-English-speaker, it was not always necessary for him to accompany me.

When Marshall Tome contracted pneumonia and could not leave his home for a month, he recorded a number of questions on tape. I later played this for my informants and they supplied the data. Obviously, this method was not as effective as having my interpreter with me, but it worked reasonably well.

The use of a tape recorder had one basic disadvantage: the transcription of tape was an exceedingly tedious procedure. It took me about four hours to transcribe one hour of tape recorded in English. At least eight hours were required to transcribe one hour of tape recorded in Navajo. It is possible, however, that my interpreter was able to make a more accurate translation of the Navajo material by working from a tape, rather than having to translate as an informant spoke.

Of course, supplementary notes were kept regarding all contacts with Navajos and all interviews having to do with Navajo activities.

Cameras were not used extensively because most of my informants were extremely reluctant to allow me to photograph them, their children, or their possessions. I attribute at least some of this shyness to the fact that most Albuquerque Navajos (including the traditionals) owned cameras, knew how to use them, and realized full well just how much information could be conveyed by good photographs.

After selecting a reliable interpreter and acquiring a tape recorder, I began my study of patterns of Navajo urban adjustment. "Adjustment" was defined in a very nebulous manner. A modified version of Spindler's (1955: 224–7) field schedule was used.

Data were gathered on the following variables: reservation background; military service; amount and source of income; type, condition, and facilities of the home; education; parental occupation, education, blood, language, and religion; religious affiliation and participation; recreational patterns; group affiliation; and idiosyncratic factors. Sociocultural adjustment pattern data were obtained through the field schedule, preliminary and supplementary notes, genealogies, and life histories. The schedule was used to implement the following aims: (1) the uniform collection of data; (2) the provision of relevant points of departure in probing the backgrounds of the various Navajos being studied; (3) the development and refinement of hypotheses; (4) the organization of data for effective analysis.

In a further attempt to present those studied in a holistic perspective, each respondent was asked to describe his activities during a "typical" day from the time he woke up in the morning until he went to sleep at night. He was also asked to describe his plans for ten or twenty years into the future.

A reasonably complete file of newspaper clippings was kept and available data relevant to the study were noted and collected. By the end of my stay in Albuquerque I had a considerable bulk of data. Notes on background research covering a wide range of subjects, a large collection of supplementary printed and mimeographed materials, AIS records, BIA materials, statistical and census reports, and a variety of other types of relevant information have been retained and filed. My master roster of Albuquerque Navajos, transcribed tape data, completed field schedules, and genealogical tables have also been filed and are available for use in future research. A card index of the 275 Albuquerque Navajos indicating all sources of collected and supplementary data for each individual serves as a master reference file. A topical file also exists.

Sixteen adult males were chosen for intensive study on the basis of their willingness to cooperate and the time I had available for field work. Impressionistically, they represent the range of Navajo types in Albuquerque. In addition, sufficient data were gathered on ninety-two others so that they could be used to test, modify, and strengthen any tentative conclusions reached based on the study of the sixteen individuals. With respect to age, marriage patterns, occupations, income, social groups, urban participation, language facility, reservation location, daily urban behavior, and migration pattern, the two aggregates appeared similar. Data from the remaining 166 Navajos were used mainly to provide depth and unity to the general demographic characterization of Navajo Albuquerque. The unavoidable strictures of the field situation and later analysis left no other alternative than to virtually ignore, for the purposes of this study, two-thirds of the Albuquerque Navajos.

In gathering data on the sixteen men, I worked in the following manner: The genealogies of the informant and his wife were taken according to the method suggested by W. H. R. Rivers (1910: 1–12). This occupied the first session. The life story was then recorded in one-hour segments. The informant was asked to begin by talking about the earliest events that he could remember, and then proceed to the present in a rough chronological order. As he talked, I referred to his genealogy and interrupted him only if he mentioned a relative not recorded in the genealogy. In the case of the non-English-speaking informants, my interpreter used the genealogy. Life stories varied in length from one-half to eight hours. The daily routine was described. I then administered the schedule.

The final phase, January, 1960, to June, 1961, was spent in editing the data. As the tapes were translated and transcribed, inconsistencies and ambiguities often appeared. I attempted to clarify these. During the period from June to July, 1960, my interpreter, my informants, and I took a welcome respite and I left the field.

Subjectively, I may say that I found this research demanding. In the first nine months of work, I drove over 10,000 miles within the city limits of Albuquerque. An average work week was eighty to ninety hours. Like *Left Handed* and *Old Mexican* (Dyk 1938, 1947) my informants, in telling me their life stories, relived them "with an intensity and vividness that was painful."

Four of my informants agreed to work with me and then changed their minds after one or two sessions, telling me either that they were "too busy" or that a *"biligana* [Anglo] really shouldn't know such things." Those who did answer all my questions, and these were in the majority, seemed quite uncomfortable at times.

I am really unable to determine why most cooperated and others did not. Financial gain did not motivate them because most Navajos agreed to be informants for nothing. I paid the traditionals $1.00 or $2.00 a session, depending upon the length of time worked. While they did appreciate the money, this was a lower rate of pay than their jobs provided.

My success, such as it was, may have been due to following the advice of a BIA school official who had worked with Indians for more than thirty years. He stated that it was impossible for an Anglo to understand fully what was "on" an Indian's mind. Therefore, I should make certain that they understood what was "on" my mind. He also strongly urged me "not to try to join them." Most Navajos would be gratified to learn that I did have a genuine interest and respect for their culture, but this interest should not be extended to the point where I identified too closely with them. Such an attitude would be interpreted as a lack of self-respect which is a cardinal sin in any Navajo's eyes.

Throughout my stay my informants frequently asked me about my attitudes, values, and manner of living. I left the field convinced that the Albuquerque Navajos had learned as much about me as I had about them.

REFERENCES

ABERLE, DAVID F.
  1961 Navajo. In *Matrilineal Kinship*, edited by D. M. Schneider and Kathleen Gough. University of California Press, Berkeley.

ABLON, JOAN
  1964 Relocated American Indians in the San Francisco Bay Area; Social Interaction and Indian Identity. *Human Organization*, Vol. 23, No. 4, pp. 296–304. Ithaca.

ADAMS, WILLIAM Y.
  1963 Shonto: A Study of the Role of the Trader in a Modern Navaho Community. *Bureau of American Ethnology, Bulletin* 188. Washington.

BEE, ROBERT L.
  1963 Changes in Yuma Social Organization. *Ethnology*, Vol. 2, No. 2, pp. 207–22. University of Pittsburgh, Pittsburgh.

BOGUE, D. J.
  1959 Internal Migration. In *The Study of Population: An Inventory and Appraisal*, edited by P. M. Hauser and O. D. Duncan, pp. 486–509. University of Chicago Press, Chicago.

CARTER, E. RUSSELL
  1953 Rapid City, South Dakota. *The American Indian*, Vol. 6, No. 4, pp. 29–38. New York.

Christian Indian
  1962 December, p. 7. Christian Reformed Church, Rehoboth.

CITY OF ALBUQUERQUE PLANNING DEPARTMENT
  1958 *Albuquerque Economic Supports Analysis*, Albuquerque.

CULLUM, ROBERT M. (Compiler)
  1957 *Assisted Navajo Relocation, 1952–1956. A Study of the Characteristics of Navajo PEOPLE who have relocated to a point away from the Navajo Reservation with Bureau of Indian Affairs Assistance.* Gallup.

DARWIN, CHARLES
  1962 *The Voyage of the Beagle*, edited by Leonard Engel. Doubleday, Garden City.

DOZIER, E. P., GEORGE E. SIMPSON AND MILTON J. YINGER
  1957 The Integration of Americans of Indian Descent. *The Annals of the American Academy of Political and Social Science*, Vol. 311, pp. 158–65. Philadelphia.

DYK, WALTER
  1938 *Son of Old Man Hat*. Harcourt, Brace and Company, New York.
  1947 A Navaho Autobiography. *Viking Fund Publications in Anthropology*, No. 8. Wenner-Gren Foundation for Anthropological Research, New York.

EBIHARA, M. M. AND G. M. KELLEY
  1955 *A Survey of the Indian Population of Portland, Oregon, in the summer of 1955*. MS, senior honors paper, Reed College, Portland.

EMPLOYMENT SECURITY REVIEW
  1959 Placing Indians Who Live on Reservations: A Cooperative Program. Vol. 26, No. 1, pp. 27–9.

FIRTH, RAYMOND
  1954 *Elements of Social Organization*. Philosophical Library, New York.

FRANCISCAN FATHERS
  1910 *An Ethnologic Dictionary of the Navaho Language*. St. Michaels.

FRANTZ, CHARLES
  1951 *The Urban Migration and Adjustment of American Indians Since 1940*. MS, master's thesis, Haverford College, Haverford.

FRED HARVEY COMPANY
 1921   Elle of Ganado, *Post Card No. 10936.*

FREILICH, MORRIS
 1958   Cultural Persistence Among the Modern Iroquois. *Anthropos,* Vol. 53, pp. 473–83. Freiburg.
 1963   Scientific Possibilities in Iroquoian Studies: An Example of Mohawks Past and Present. *Anthropologica,*
         N.S., Vol. 5, No. 2, pp. 171–86. Ottawa.

GETTY, HARRY THOMAS
 1950   *Interethnic Relationships in the Community of Tucson.* MS, doctoral dissertation, University of Chicago,
         Chicago.

GLUCKMAN, MAX (EDITOR)
 1964   *Closed Systems and Open Minds: The Limits of Naivety in Social Anthropology.* Aldine, Chicago.

GOLDSCHMIDT, WALTER
 1959   *Man's Way: A Preface to the Understanding of Human Society.* Holt, Rinehart and Winston, New York.

GRIFFITH, CHARLES R.
 1960   *Navaho Intercultural Marriage: A Study of Acculturation in Small Groups.* MS, doctoral dissertation,
         Harvard University, Cambridge.

HANSON, MARSHALL R.
 1960   *Plains Indians and Urbanization.* MS, doctoral dissertation, Stanford University, Palo Alto.

HAURY, EMIL W. (EDITOR)
 1954   *American Anthropologist,* Vol. 56, No. 4, Part 1. Menasha.

HAWLEY, FLORENCE
 1948   *Some Factors in the Indian Problem in New Mexico.* Division of Research, Department of Govern-
         ment, University of New Mexico, Albuquerque.

HENING, H. B. AND E. D. JOHNSON
 1908   *Albuquerque, New Mexico.* Press of *The Albuquerque Morning Journal.*

HILLERY, GEORGE A. AND FRANK J. ESSENE
 1963   Navajo Population: An Analysis of the 1960 Census. *Southwestern Journal of Anthropology,* Vol. 19,
         No. 3, 1963. Albuquerque.

HIRABAYASHI, JAMES A.
 1964   A Social Survey of American Indian Urban Integration. MS in possession of author, San Francisco
         State College.

HODGE, WILLIAM H.
 1964   Navaho Pentecostalism. *Anthropological Quarterly,* Vol. 37, No. 3, pp. 73–93. Washington.
 1967   Navaho Urban Silversmiths. *Anthropological Quarterly,* Vol. 40, No. 4, pp. 185–200. Washington.

HUCKLE, JOHN F. (EDITOR)
 1928   *American Indians, First Families of the Southwest.* 4th ed., Fred Harvey, Kansas City.

HURT, WESLEY R., JR.
 1961-62   The Urbanization of the Yankton Indians. *Human Organization,* Vol. 20, No. 4, pp. 226–31. Ithaca.

KLUCKHOHN, CLYDE
 1963   *Navaho Witchcraft.* Beacon Press, Boston.

KLUCKHOHN, CLYDE AND DOROTHEA C. LEIGHTON
 1946   *The Navaho.* Harvard University Press, Cambridge.

KROEBER, THEODORA
 1961   *Ishi in Two Worlds.* University of California Press, Berkeley.

KURTZ, RONALD J.
 1963   *Role Change and Culture Change: The Canyoncito Case.* MS, doctoral dissertation, University of New
         Mexico, Albuquerque.

LANGE, CHARLES H.
 1959   *Cochiti, A New Mexico Pueblo, Past and Present.* University of Texas Press, Austin.

LEIGHTON, DOROTHEA AND CLYDE KLUCKHOHN
 1948   *Children of the People.* Harvard University Press, Cambridge.

LESSER, ALEXANDER
 1961   Social Fields and the Evolution of Society. *Southwestern Journal of Anthropology,* Vol. 17, No. 1,
         pp. 40–8. Albuquerque.

LOVRICH, FRANK
1952 *The Assimilation of the Indian in Rapid City.* MS, master's thesis, University of South Dakota, Vermillion.

LUEBBEN, RALPH AUGUST
1955 *A Study of Some off-reservation Navaho Miners.* MS, doctoral dissertation, Cornell University, Ithaca.
1964 Prejudice and Discrimination Against Navahos in a Mining Community. *The Kiva,* Vol. 30, No. 1, pp. 1–17. Tucson.

MacGREGOR, GORDON
1946 *Warriors Without Weapons.* University of Chicago Press, Chicago.

MADIGAN, LaVERNE
1956 *The American Indian Relocation Program.* Association on American Indian Affairs, New York.

MANN, ALBERT Z.
1957 *A Mission to Indian Americans in the City. The Summary Report of a Survey of the Work of the United Church Committee Among Indian People Resettling in the Twin Cities.* Minneapolis.

MANZOLILLO, LOLA R.
1955 *The American Indian in an Urban Situation: Minneapolis, Minnesota. A Study in Applied Anthropology.* MS, master's thesis, University of Minnesota, Minneapolis.

MARTIN, HARRY W.
1964 Correlates of Adjustment Among American Indians in an Urban Environment. *Human Organization,* Vol. 23, No. 4, pp. 290–5. Ithaca.

MERIAM, LEWIS (EDITOR)
1928 *The Problem of Indian Administration.* Institute for Government Research, The Johns Hopkins Press, Baltimore.

McKINNEY, LILLIE
1934 *History of the Albuquerque Indian School.* MS, master's thesis, University of New Mexico, Albuquerque.

McPHEE, J. C. (COMPILER)
1953 *Indians in non-Indian Communities. A Survey of Living Conditions Among Navajo and Hopi Indians Residing in Gallup, N. M., Farmington, N. M., Cortez, Colo., Winslow, Ariz., Flagstaff, Ariz., Holbrook, Ariz.* The Window Rock Area, U. S. Indian Service, Welfare Placement Branch. Window Rock.

MITCHELL, J.
1949 The Mohawks in High Steel. *The New Yorker,* Vol. 25, No. 30, pp. 38–52. New York.

NAVAJO TIMES
1960-65 Window Rock.

NEW MEXICO STATE EMPLOYMENT SERVICE
1961 *A Study of Migration and Migrant Characteristics.* New Mexico State Employment Service, Research Unit. Albuquerque.

PARKER, SEYMOUR
1954 *Navaho Adjustment to Town Life: A Preliminary Report on the Navahos Residing in Farmington.* MS, Cornell Southwest Project, Ithaca.

PARSONS, ELSIE CLEWS
1932 Isleta, New Mexico. *Forty-Seventh Annual Report of the Bureau of American Ethnology,* pp. 191–466. Washington.

RITZENTHALER, ROBERT AND MARY SELLERS
1955 Indians in an Urban Situation. *Wisconsin Archaeologist,* Vol. 36, No. 4, pp. 147–61. Milwaukee.

RIVERS, W. H. R.
1910 The Genealogical Method of Anthropological Inquiry. *Sociological Review,* Vol. 3, pp. 1–12. Manchester.

SASAKI, TOM T.
1960 *Fruitland, New Mexico: A Navaho Community in Transition.* Cornell University Press, Ithaca.

SEARS, PAUL M.
1954 Gallup Merchants Like It — When Indians Come to Town. Reprint from *New Mexico Business,* Bureau of Business Research, University of New Mexico, Albuquerque.

SHEPARDSON, MARY
1961 *Factionalism in a Navajo Community.* Paper read at the 1961 meetings of the Southwestern Anthropological Association, Berkeley.

SHEPARDSON, MARY AND BLODWEN HAMMOND
    1964   Change and Persistence in an Isolated Navajo Community. *American Anthropologist,* Vol. 66, No. 5, pp. 1029–50. Menasha.

SLOTKIN, JAMES S.
    1957   *The Menomini Powwow.* Milwaukee Public Museum, Publications in Anthropology, No. 4, Milwaukee.

SPICER, EDWARD H.
    1940   *Pascua, A Yaqui Village in Arizona.* University of Chicago Press, Chicago.
    1962   *Cycles of Conquest.* University of Arizona Press, Tucson.

SPINDLER, GEORGE D.
    1955   *Sociocultural and Psychological Processes in Menomini Acculturation.* University of California Press, Berkeley.

STANLEY, F.
    1963   *The Duke City: The Story of Albuquerque, New Mexico, 1706–1956.* Pampa Print Shop, Pampa.

UNDERHILL, RUTH
    1953   *Here Come the Navaho!* U. S. Indian Service, Haskell Institute, Lawrence.

UNITED STATES GOVERNMENT
    1960   *U. S. Census of Population: 1960.* U. S. Bureau of the Census, U. S. Government Printing Office. Washington.

VAN VALKENBURGH, RICHARD F.
    1941   *Dine Bikeyah.* U.S. Office of Indian Affairs, Navajo Service, Window Rock.

VERDET, PAULA
    1961   *Summary of Research on Indians in St. Louis and Chicago.* Mimeod sheet, Monteith College, Wayne State University, Detroit.

WHITE, LESLIE A.
    1962   The Pueblo of Sia, New Mexico. *Bureau of American Ethnology, Bulletin 184.* Washington.

WHITE, ROBERT
    1962   *The Urban Adjustment of the Dakota Indians in Rapid City: A Progress Report.* Mimeod, Rapid City.

YOUNG, ROBERT W. (EDITOR)
    1961   *The Navajo Yearbook, 1951–1961: A Decade of Progress. Report No. VIII.* Window Rock.

ZICKEFOOSE, PAUL W.
    1962   Economic Survey of Gallup, New Mexico, 1950–1960, of a Highway Relocation Impact Study: The "Before" Portion. *New Mexico Highway Department Bulletin* 24. University Park.